THERE'S A SNAKE IN MY GARDEN

JILL BRISCOE

MONARCH
BOOKS

Oxford, UK & Grand Rapids, Michigan, USA

Text copyright © 2008 Jill Briscoe

The right of Jill Briscoe to be identified as the author of this work has been asserted by her in accordance with the Copyright, Designs and Patents Act 1988.

Originally published in the United States of America by Zondervan in 1975; revised edition 2000, Shaw; updated edition 2008.

Published in association with the literary agency of Alive Communications, Inc., 7680 Goddard Street, Suite 200, Colorado Springs, CO 80920.

Published in the UK by Monarch Books
an imprint of
Lion Hudson plc
Wilkinson House, Jordan Hill Road,
Oxford OX2 8DR, England
Email: monarch@lionhudson.com
www.lionhudson.com/monarch

ISBN: 978-1-85424-839-8
e-ISBN: 978-0-85721-423-2

This edition 2008

Acknowledgments
Unless otherwise stated, Scripture quotations are taken from the Holy Bible, New International Version, © 1973, 1978, 1984 by the International Bible Society. Used by permission of Hodder & Stoughton Ltd. All rights reserved.

Cover art by Jen Warren.

A catalogue record for this book is available from the British Library.

TO STUART

who keeps my mind on the Lord,
my feet on the ground,
and my heart in his love.

Contents

Foreword

When one has enjoyed two people as we have enjoyed Stuart and Jill Briscoe and been helped by their biblical ministry as we have been helped, one is more than interested to read something about their own spiritual pilgrimage. Being a woman, I wanted to know more about this remarkable woman and what makes her tick. I expected something honest, humourous, inspirational and challenging. It was all that and more.

Ruth B. Graham

"The serpent was the craftiest of all the creatures the Lord God had made" (Genesis 3:1, TLB).

The Snake

Did you ever hear of Satan – or are you an
    unbeliever?
Did you ever laugh deridingly and prove him
    archdeceiver?
Did you ever hear of Calvary and shrug – "Why should
    I care"?
Did you ever care that God's one Son was mutilated
    there?
Did you ever see an empty cross and face an empty
    tomb?
Did you know he rose the victor o'er the snake and
    hell and doom?
Did you ever join his army, did you ever take your
    shield?
Did you ever march out sword in hand onto the
    battlefield?
Did you ever find the ranks grow thin the worse the
    fight became?
Did you ever watch men in retreat: the blind, the halt,
    the lame?
Did you ever notice nearer Christ the arrows thicker
    land?
Did you ever see the impact in his side, his feet, his
    hand?
Did you ever fully realise that Christ died without
    protection?

That you may have his armour, not act traitor by
   defection?
Did you ever wonder why he waits and tolerates
   lukewarmness?
And your pitiful rebellion and your coldness and your
   hardness?
And your casual indifference and your hunger for
   possessions?
Did you know he stops the arrows by his constant
   intercessions?
Did you ever thank your Jesus, did it ever break your
   heart?
Did you ever go out fighting and decide to play your
   part?
If you ever get around to war and put your armour
   on,
Then the snake will be defeated to the glory of God's
   Son.

1

Behind the Smile

I always believed in God, that Jesus Christ was his Son, and that the Bible was true. My parents taught me the difference between right and wrong. Right was being "good", which would make me and everyone else happy; wrong was being "bad", which would make me and everyone else sad. Why, then, did I find myself wanting to be bad instead of good? Why did wrongdoing bring me enjoyment? Why was being "good" dull and boring? Maybe someone had given me the wrong information.

Everything in my garden was lovely. Any legitimate tree was mine to enjoy: the tree of education; the tree of recreation; the tree of travel; the trees of fine friendships and wholesome entertainment; the precious trees of a loving family and carefree days. Of these I freely ate. But like Eve, I found myself desiring to possess above all others the fruit from the one tree I was forbidden to touch!

As for Eve, so for me. The forbidden tree stood among the forest of permitted things. Daily it reminded me of one of God's choicest gifts to human beings created in his image – the gift of my free will.

I didn't know it then, but along with the trees in my garden there was also a snake. He came to me as he came to Eve – in familiar form – for his devices have never changed. He spoke to me through people I'd known all my life; my friends who lived in the garden, too, so I was not alarmed or suspicious.

"Eat the fruit. We have, and we didn't drop dead!" So I took it, too, because I had to know what it tasted like. I didn't realise that the process of death begins with the first bite; by the time the fruit is finished, you begin to feel pretty sick.

I loved and respected my parents too much to hurt them. But I felt they wouldn't understand my rationalising my sin and calling it "growing up". So I decided the best thing to do was to pretend to be "good" when they were around. Meanwhile, I learned to eat my fruit in parts of the garden inhabited only by the snake and myself!

For example, I knew I shouldn't read dirty books, so I didn't. But dirty thoughts were better and could be indulged in behind the smile. I'd been told it was wrong to cheat at exams, but I could dispense with my guilt by arguing that cheating made for better grades, and better grades for happier parents – as long as I wasn't caught! But what if I was? Well, then I could always chloroform my conscience and lie myself out of the situation. Wouldn't that be kinder than telling the truth, which would cause hurt and embarrassment to those I loved?

By now I was eighteen and becoming increasingly confused. I was definitely not fulfilled. Something or someone was still missing. I looked around at others. Had they discovered the secret of life? Sometimes I got behind their smiles and saw reality. One of the wealthiest men I knew committed suicide. Material things obviously hadn't helped him fill the void. My sick friend in the hospital wasn't happy, but she blamed her health problem. I had my health, so that wasn't the answer either. Another friend wasn't satisfied, tossed to and fro as she was between parents with marriage problems. Yet living as I was in the midst of love, generated by my parents' happy marriage, I still knew insecurity.

Somehow I sensed that the answer lay not in material things or even in the enjoyment of the good things in life such as health and happiness, but somewhere in the mystical, moral realm – the "good" and the "bad" bit! But goodness seemed so hard to define, and badness had begun to make me sick of myself, so where was the answer? What did I have to do? Where did I have to go? How good did I need to become, or how bad did I have to be to find – what? In my confusion, I didn't know what I was looking for. Maybe "it" was waiting for me in another garden, a new environment.

My chance came to prove the point when I was accepted at a teachers' training college at Cambridge.

"Yes," I assured the interviewer, "I love little children," while behind the smile the snake snickeringly hissed, "You do?!"

Once established at college, the snake's cynicism proved correct. Little children were soon categorised in my mind as so much necessary nuisance value. They made demands on my precious, trivia-filled time that I needed for my headlong rush to find new trees laden with fruit I had never dared to taste in my beautifully protected garden back home.

I majored in drama and art, which helped me to project the smile and perform whatever role it suited my selfish interest to play. Many women have abilities in this direction. Speech is a constant part of their existence, and drama helps to make them the stimulating, or aggravating, inveterate role players that they can be. I was apparently good at both, expecting others to be as impressed with my performance as I was! My life now became like one long "play", in every sense of the word. Before the curtains drew back and revealed me, I was alone, frightened, unsure of how I would relate to the crowd. Would they like the things I did? Would they laugh at my lines, cry at the pathos, and applaud my wild attention-getting antics? It was terribly important to me to know that I'd pleased them. Back in the dressing room with the makeup off, the costumes laid aside, what exhaustion, depression and unfulfilled feelings were mine.

Perhaps there had been too many performances, or maybe I had just eaten too much bad fruit. I didn't know. Anyway, a mysterious stomach ailment took me to the hospital. Behind the smile I was terrified. I needed answers to my questions now. No longer was my major concern to fill a selfish life or get my own way, but how to deal with fear, cope with pain, look at the suffering of others and find a relevant comforting word. I had to grapple with the reality of death and find an answer.

I discovered that when I was flat on my back, there was only one way to look. Up! That's where I'd always believed God was to be found. But what do you say to a stranger who may not even be aware of the infinitesimal smudge of a mess lying in an obscure pinprick of a hospital bed on Planet Earth?

"Help!" I said. "Make me better. Get me out of here! Quick, stop the pain. Are you receiving me?" O dear, that made him sound like a radio. Radio or not, he picked up the message and placed a great transmitter next to my left ear.

Her name was Jenny, and she lay in the bed next to mine. She it was who told me that I had a snake in my garden, that I'd listened to his every word and believed his lies instead of God's truth. The fruit looked so good that I'd eaten it. I'd wanted to be wise and had finished up conceited and arrogant. I'd been my own god, but now I couldn't even answer my own prayers! No wonder I was sick in soul. My sin found me wearing fig-leaf arguments, carefully stitched but painfully inadequate.

"Jesus came and died on the cross for you, Jill," Jenny told me. "There he bruised the serpent's head and defeated him, but not before the snake had bruised his heel so that he suffered dreadfully. He rose again triumphant over death and sin and is alive. He wants to come into your life by his Holy Spirit."

"What's his Holy Spirit?" I asked. I had heard of the Holy Ghost, but his name had conjured up a picture of a sheet-shrouded spook who haunted old English churches! In my ignorant opinion he was left free to do so because evidently God had either died or gone on vacation, leaving behind his ghostly janitor. Jenny laughed. Did Christians laugh? I thought they were far too morbid and dreary and pious for that! But apparently I was wrong.

"The Holy Spirit was his divine nature released at Pentecost," she explained. "The Holy Spirit makes it possible for you to possess the very life of Christ."

The smile forgotten, tears flowed as, exposed in my garden and convicted of my sin, I accepted God's covering for my nakedness. Clothed in his forgiveness and his grace I turned around to walk away from the tree of disobedience to a new life.

The snake in my garden writhed in fury and slithered out of sight – for a while!

2

The Shiniest Locker
in the Ward

My bedside locker boasted the shiniest top in the hospital ward. Jenny had begun to "follow me up", and polishing my locker top was a good excuse for the Christian nurses on the ward to visit me! A pretty, dark-haired nurse with twinkling blue eyes (were all Christians as pretty as this? I'd thought they were all dowdy, bun-bedecked, long-skirted frumps!) asked me brightly, "Did something important happen yesterday?" Another young woman inquired, "You're looking happy today. How's that?" Yet another took a much more direct approach, "Jenny says that you have something to tell me!"

I didn't know it, but Jenny was making sure I got plenty of practice giving my testimony! I had never heard of such a thing or read the verse in the Bible that says, "If you confess with your mouth, 'Jesus is Lord,' and believe in your heart that God raised him from the dead, you will be saved" (Romans 10:9). But Jenny had knowledge of this and knew the value of confession.

What did I have to confess after two days? About the only thing I could say was that Jesus was Lord instead of me. That much I knew. I had asked him into my life to rule and to direct, and I knew he was there. How did I know? Was it a feeling? No, it was deeper than a feeling, bigger than an emotion; it was an inner conviction. I was convinced with inner certainty that I belonged to Jesus and that he belonged to me. As the Bible says in Romans 8:16, "The Spirit himself testifies with our spirit that we are God's children." It was God's Spirit telling my spirit that he had arrived.

What did I have to tell after two days? I could tell these new friends that I knew I'd been forgiven. I tried to tell the dark-haired little nurse, but it was hard to find the words. The love and gratefulness and tears kept getting in the way! There had been so much to forgive. "The one that is forgiven much loves much," she said quietly. "That's what Jesus said." She was right. To my amazement I loved him already, and love for these new friends overwhelmed me, too. I was so glad to learn I wasn't the only one in the world who needed forgiveness and a new birth. There were others who had experienced the same thing. How many of them were there?

I lay in bed that night thinking back to the girls at college. Suddenly I began to understand those students with a special light in their eyes, spring in their step, and wholeness of life. later I learned it was holiness. For so long they had mystified me and made me feel uneasy. But now I understood them – they were Christians. How could I go back and expect them to accept me? Especially that one girl I had taken delight in embarrassing in a drama production when my part had involved so much blasphemy and innuendo, and she had responded. And then there was that senior student. I thought about the day I had so rudely burst into her room with a message and found her on her knees. She wasn't even embarrassed to be discovered looking so stupid praying beside her bed like a baby. I was the one who felt awkward and annoyed with her!

I must also face my friends. Late into the night I lay thinking about them. What were they going to say? I thought I knew the answer to that. They would say what I would have said if the roles had been reversed. How could I answer their questions if they ever gave me the opportunity of answering them? I didn't even have a Bible.

The next morning I found a new Bible lying on my highly polished locker top. Eager, loving friends had bought it for me. I knew the answers I needed were contained inside, but I did wish it were a little smaller! It seemed so prominent perched there in full view of the ward. Ashamed of my ingratitude, I determined not to care. In fact, I decided I would leave it in full view when my friends came to visit me. However, my courage departed abruptly when I saw them swinging noisily down the ward in my direction, and I hastily covered it up with a magazine. Jenny sent one of her nurse friends over to meet my friends. The nurse removed the magazine, saying casually, "Can I borrow this for Jenny?" I knew Jenny didn't want to read it; she was helping me tell my friends. Now they saw the Bible. They would have had to be suffering from a severe case of glaucoma to avoid doing so! The conversation became a little awkward. Sidelong glances were exchanged, and with stilted wishes for my recovery they took their leave.

"Jenny, I'll lose them," I lamented.

"What sort of friends are they if they ditch you because you've found God?" she asked me. "Anyway, if you do lose them, God will give you new friends."

"But I don't want new friends. I want my old ones. Does being a Christian mean I'll have to stop doing things with them and stop going to the places I'm used to going to? What will I have to give up?"

I'll never forget her answer. "God will only ask you to give up those activities and habits that are going to do you harm, and you'll know what those things are. He'll tell you."

"How will he tell me, Jenny? I don't know what I should or shouldn't do. I don't know where or where not to go. I don't know anything!"

"Here you are in the hospital. You think you have been laid aside by illness, but you haven't. You've been called aside for stillness. So, get your nose in this Bible and start."

"But how? Where do I start, and what do I read? How will I understand and know I'm interpreting it correctly?"

"Jesus said, 'The Holy Spirit will guide you into all truth.' He'll take his Word and make it make sense to you. Start in the New Testament with the Gospel of John."

She dug into a big handbag hanging on the end of the bed and produced numerous booklets which she gave me to read: *Becoming a Christian* and *Being a Christian* by the Reverend John R. W. Stott explained simply just what had happened to me and encouraged me to seek to grow as a baby Christian by desiring the "purse spiritual milk" (1 Peter 2:2).

"Now, then, you're going to need to start having some quiet time with God," Jenny announced.

I eagerly agreed! The sound of the battle ahead convinced me I needed to escape from my responsibilities and my problems to some cave of solitude. But apparently "escape" was not the idea behind a "quiet time". The idea was to open one's ears to the still, small voice that would keep asking the simple question, "What are you doing here?" The owner of the voice would listen to all my excuses and then command me to depart from my cave into the battle, fortified and encouraged by my time alone with him.

"Start with fifteen minutes a day," I was instructed. "Read a portion of the Bible; these notes will help you," she said, giving me some daily Bible helps. "Then pray about what you read. Look for commands to obey, promises to claim, warnings to heed, and answers to your questions. At the end of your daily time with God, start learning these verses." Then she handed me a little packet put out by The Navigators with verses of Scripture to memorise printed out on little cards.

"There are 48 in each packet. I'll listen to them as you learn them!" Then she produced three large books from somewhere under her bedcovers. "Read these in your spare time. They are adventure stories of people who became Christians and went about turning the world upside down." My shiny locker top had disappeared under a pile of books, booklets and the Bible. I thought of the "called aside for stillness" and the "quiet time" and smiled at the irony of the terms! But I got the message: I'd better get to work.

During the remaining days in the hospital I read the story of Daniel. The story of the lions' den was not news to me, but the story of Daniel refusing to eat the king's meat was. As I read the story in one of my first quiet times, the Holy Spirit took the truth and applied it. "Jill, I want you to set a goal in your heart not to defile yourself with the king's meat!" God was telling me forbidden fruit was out. He was teaching me that anything which would defile my relationship with the Holy Spirit was not to be eaten. If I would say "no", then when the time came to enter the den of lions (I had an immediate vision of my friends with hairy manes and wide mouths waiting to gobble me up!), God would shut their mouths. God would prove himself not only to me, but also to others who might be watching.

When I talked to Jenny later about the friend issue, she said, "Of course you may win them to Christ, and then you won't lose them."

"Me?!"

"Yes, you!" said Jenny, ignoring my incredulity. "Jesus Christ is a great soul-winner, and he's come into your life to use your body as a ship from which to fish."

"Help!" I thought, wondering how long it would take the good Lord to discover I was more like a leaky sieve than a sturdy trawler.

As if she had read my thoughts, Jenny commented that God liked cracked, broken vessels best. That way he, the Great Fisherman, got the glory. She then showed me 1 Corinthians 1:26–29 and pointed out that as I was foolish, weak, lowly and despised I was just the vessel he was looking for! That was all right, then. He would surely gain much glory by using me!

"How do I lead them to Christ?" I asked.

"Tell them what I told you," she said. "Use these verses: Romans 3:23 – the fact of sin; Romans 6:23 – the penalty of sin; John 3:16 – Jesus died for sinners; Revelation 3:20 – you must receive him. Ask them if they believe this. If they say 'yes', ask them if they know how to receive him. If they answer in the negative, ask them if they would like you to help them by praying a prayer they could repeat and make their own, like the one we prayed together. Do you remember?"

I remembered. My memory wasn't as bad as that; it was only a week ago! I wrote it down in the back of my Bible along with the Bible verses. I was getting my fishing equipment ready!

3

Let's Go Fishing

few days later the intrepid fisherman, clutching her rod cautiously, approached the muddied streams of college where the "big fish" were to be found.

Jenny had been at it again! She had let the other Christian fishermen know I was on my way. To my amazement all sorts of strangers became my friends immediately, including the girl in the drama incident and the senior student at college! It was a whole new world. We shared the same life, the same goals, and the same commission. Jesus had said, "Come after me and I will make you fishers of men." I learned quickly that although we were doing the same thing, each of us had to catch our own fish. I could be excited over my sister's catch, but I could also expect a fish of my own, even though I was so new and inexperienced. (After all, little boys just starting out with a stick and a bent pin expect to catch something!) Jenny had told me to make myself available to the Lord day by day and watch to see whose company I was thrown into. I was to listen for any stray remark I could use as an opportunity; then I could invite the one I believed God was bringing across my path to coffee and lead her to Christ! It sounded so easy. I prayed. I watched. I listened, expecting to be led to someone needing Jesus. Sure enough, I was!

"Would you come to coffee tonight, Audrey?"

"Sure," she replied.

"Help, Lord! She accepted, now what?" I reported to the Big Fisherman.

God was good to me. Audrey was full of questions.

"Jill, what's happened to you? Are you going to a nunnery or something?" With my heart beating wildly, I answered as best I knew how, read the verses to her, and asked her if she believed.

"Yes, I do," she replied seriously.

Now came the big question, "Will you pray with me to accept Christ?" But I couldn't ask it. What if it didn't work? How foolish we'd look. Maybe it was enough to influence her! I had an immediate picture of my father, an ardent salmon fisherman, announcing at the end of a day's fishing, "Well, I influenced a lot of fish today!" No, I knew I had to catch her. So I asked the all-important question, "Will you accept Jesus Christ as your Saviour and Lord?"

"Yes," she replied. "Oh, Jill, yes."

We knelt; we prayed. I peeked between my fingers in hope and fear. What I saw convinced me that another miracle had happened. Triumphantly I paid my visit to Jenny with Audrey in tow. Instead of the expected congratulations, I received immediate orders!

Now that I had become a spiritual mother (and at such a young age too!), I had to take my responsibility seriously. My job was to feed the new spiritual baby by helping her to read the Bible and have a quiet time. I needed to protect her by prayer and encouragement. Then I could help her to lead another to Christ. After this I must see to it that she became a good spiritual parent, and so on ad infinitum!

The future stretched before me bright with promise. I had never experienced a thrill comparable to seeing heaven open to my friend Audrey: to watch one forgiven much and see her beginning to love much; to see how God began to answer my prayers and her prayers, changing lives, dissipating loneliness, giving purpose and direction; to be a blessing to those closest to me was thrilling. How I longed for everyone to know him.

Most people who fish have many tales of "the one that got away!" My best friend was one such fish. We shared a room during our first year in college, and not wishing to embarrass her (that was my excuse!), I asked a Christian friend if I might have my quiet time in the sanctuary of her room. Never will I forget the day she firmly said, "Jill, you go to your own room and have it there!"

"Oh, but I can't," I protested as the door closed firmly and finally behind me. "Help, Lord, be reasonable," I complained. "I can't kneel and pray in front of her. She'll misunderstand and it won't help you at all!" The battle raged. I thought of Daniel praying three times a day with his window open even when he knew the opposition was peeking in – and that meant the lions! I wondered why he didn't shut the windows.

Then I realised that was just what I had been doing – shutting the windows!

At last I knelt. I couldn't pray, but it didn't matter. It was enough to be there. Steps came along the corridor. I never realised before how short the corridor was! The door swung open. Silence. Unbelieving silence. Then a gasp as the door slammed, and my friend retired to spread the news that she was living with a religious fanatic. She never spoke to me again, even though we lived together for the rest of the year.

I complained to my Master about the oppressive silence. "Well," said the Lord, "you prayed that I would shut the lion's mouth; now be satisfied!"

I understood my roommate's scorn and disgust. She knew me so well. She believed I had to be pretending, and this understandably was the height of hypocrisy.

I visited the hospital and poured out my distress to Jenny, who listened but gave me little sympathy. She renewed her simple challenge to me to let my life speak. She gave me assurance by sharing many of her tales of the "one that got away". Sometimes they ended up on another fishing rod, she said, so I just had to pray, commit my friend to him, and let him deal with the hurt.

Jenny's health improved. It was time for her to leave the hospital and me. I was glad she was well, but wished God would keep her around a little longer. Couldn't the Lord arrange a simple appendectomy or something? What would I do without her? But God knew I had her on a spiritual pedestal, and it was time to rely on him alone, not on any crutch, however precious.

"What happens if I fall?" I wailed.

"Oh, you'll fall!" she replied cheerfully. "What toddler doesn't? Just get up and try again. There's never been a healthy baby who hasn't learned to walk with practice!"

I remembered those words in the days that followed. Days after the first thrill had left me and I couldn't feel his presence, I remembered that a loving parent removes his support to teach his child to walk in obedience. That was a hard lesson, but I was growing up.

I returned to the hospital once more before they discovered my ailment and remedied it. There was a girl in the ward who had had the same serious bone operation that Jenny had had and who was in great pain. Being allowed to move around the ward, I longed to help. How? The idea came straight from heaven. Her locker top! I was there in a flash tidying it up, leaving her a booklet, soothing her brow, loving her already before she became my sister in Christ. That night after she became a new person, I prayed, "I'm a leaky vessel, but thank you for coming on board, Captain. I'm a lousy fisherman, but keep up the lessons. I'm learning. Thank you for helping me to discover a gift: I can polish locker tops."

Bugs

Wouldn't it be lovely if a bug could stay always
Warm inside its silk cocoon, protected all its days
Alone in dark oblivion, no need to fly the skies?
Let's face it – God's rebellious world's no place for
     butterflies.

Now God, he made these little bugs and placed within
    his life
So growth, the natural evidence, brings strain and
    stress and strife;
For as she grows the cozy case becomes a prison
    strong,
The bug now knows she *must* break out; to stay a bug
    is *wrong*.

At last the struggle over – the butterfly is free
to fly God's earth upheld by him in matchless
    symmetry.
Cries watching man in God's lost world, *"A Miracle is
    this,*
From crumpled bug to butterfly" –
God's metamorphosis.

4

Arranged, Strange or Deranged

Having graduated from college, I began teaching in my hometown of Liverpool. I taught first year students, loved my work, and had plenty of free time for the King's business. Someone said, "The mission field is between your own two feet." If that were true, part of my commission lay within the four walls of my classroom. First year students? Well, they surely needed a changed nature, sweet though they were! I never had to teach them to answer back, be rude, selfish or stubborn; all that appeared to come quite naturally. I decided it would help if I had someone within their group on my side as I struggled to teach not only the first steps of maths and English, but also priorities of life.

My problem was that I was not the teacher he wanted me to be, and for a simple reason: I could not control my temper. Fresh out of college and believing in the "new" concept of free choice, I sought to put into practice all I had learned. The basis of this concept was that the children should be free to choose exactly what they wanted to do. As learning comes through doing, they would learn more quickly by "choosing" to work at maths and English instead of being "made" to do things they disliked.

"Now, children, maths or art today?" I inquired in a cheerful voice. Paintbrushes and easels ran out while I was left holding a pile of maths materials. "Reading or the playhouse?" I made a mental note that we would need a new playhouse soon. Due to overcrowding it was due for demolition! "Watch the rabbits, stick bugs and mice, children! Try not to step on them," I pleaded. "Johnny, did you try to teach Mickey Mouse to swim today? What do you mean you had a burial service in the sandbox?"

The climax came one day when I discovered a game of hospital in progress. Some nice little boys were playing out their frustrations by taking out a friend's tonsils with a pair of scissors. Just as I made this discovery, a child tripped over the leg of a chair and fell against a paint easel, emptying pots of paint the entire length of the classroom. I felt that if the children were allowed freedom to create as they wished, so was the teacher. I created – and how!

Later, at home, I knelt and asked forgiveness. This had to be beaten. How could I serve him when there was a part of my life constantly being defeated? Was I supposed to live with defeat because I couldn't be perfect? I read the answer in Romans 6:14: "Sin shall not be your master." But it had been!

How disappointed the Lord must be! Miserably I struggled to gain control over my temper at school. Day after day I returned defeated to pray the same prayer, "Forgive me, Lord, I did it again." If there was no victory in the Christian life, just what did Christ offer? If only I could feel he understood. But I had this foreboding that he stood in the corner of my classroom, loving the children, cross with me, and ready to rebuke and condemn the moment I transgressed.

At that time I read a story about a lighthouse keeper who broke a window in his lighthouse. Believing no ships were in the area, he filled in the aperture with a board. The light shone brightly from all sides except one. There was only one "part dark". Surely it wouldn't matter. That night a ship approaching the lighthouse on the dark side was shipwrecked. The moral: There must be no "part dark". I knew this. No matter how much his light was shining out of other areas of my life, this temper part was dark; it was tripping up those to whom I was seeking to witness at school. I was not to settle for defeat. This (I learned from my Bible) was not normal Christianity.

I searched the Scriptures for an answer. In Hebrews 4:15 I read that he "has been tempted in every way, just as we are – yet was without sin"! If it said in *all* points, it meant in *all* points. In other words, he understood the pressure! He was not standing in the corner of my classroom waiting to condemn, but in the person of the Holy Spirit he had come alongside to help. In fact, he was saying, "Aren't they little beasts! How frustrating they are even though we love them so much! I understand. I stood among my children here on earth and watched the chaos created by freedom without discipline! You're going to need more patience than mere human patience, more love than you are capable of. Let me give you mine; for love, patience and self-control are the products of my work within you." I needed to appreciate and appropriate those divine qualities.

Soon I learned to mix freedom with discipline and, drawing on his resources, I knew victory at last. Many of those little children found the Saviour and gave me good practice in breaking the Bread of Life small enough for them to digest. What a message we Christians have to give to the world! There must be no "part dark".

Now I felt I should join a group of Christians and help them get the message out. I had so much to share about how Christ can overcome. But which group should I join? I began looking for a fellowship of believers. I discovered that Christians appeared to be divided into three categories: the arranged, the strange or the deranged!

The *arranged* were just that. Religious routine rolled monotonously along taking them with it. These people usually sat in the same pew every week, wore hats to church, carried big Bibles, taught Sunday school, and cut up sandwiches for ladies' teas. Rigid rules abounded. Conforming to their physical image, I removed all my makeup, resulting in the most irritating inquiries as to the state of my health. My hair was cropped like a boy's to avoid vanity. It did! I lowered my skirts to regulation lengths, which had dangerous repercussions since I was driving a motor scooter at the time. I learned all the right choruses to sing at the after-church fellowship. This fellowship consisted of party games, which made me feel rather stupid having last played such games when I was thirteen. But this was apparently how Christians had fun. Then we had a few choruses (which also appeared rather childish) and a five-minute epilogue delivered in an apologetic manner, as if the person presenting the Word wished he didn't have to bring Christ into it. I observed that most of the young people left before the epilogue!

I was soon bored with it all. This wasn't getting the message out! Sunday after Sunday those of us who were saved listened to a message on how to be saved, while those who were lost continued unaware of their plight, far removed from the preacher's voice.

I looked around and decided to join the *strange* group! This group of Christians had decided that the arranged group was for the old fogies and not for "in-touch-with-the-Lord, go-ahead" folk like them! Bible texts poured from their lips. They rushed about on street corners giving out tracts. They were *determined* to be a blessing and were always ready to tell you (with humility) how many drunks had accepted Christ through them last night, or how they had spent the whole night in prayer! They scoffed at established church services and sang hymns in public places, even if they had voices that sounded like cinders grating. Although I had some misgivings about many of the pushier parts of their outreach, I never dared to voice them in case I should be considered unspiritual.

I threw myself into the programme. It was certainly exciting and a lot more fun than the arranged group! I learned how to reach the tough "Teddy boys" through street meetings. One of them even gave me his flick knife as a keepsake. I painted chairs and scrubbed floors at the Chinese Gospel Mission in a seedy part of Liverpool. I preached from the precarious pulpit of a rowboat to people having picnics along the riverside and stood on upturned crates on bomb sites enjoying my first taste of open-air preaching. (This last activity was brought to an abrupt halt when my headteacher from school joined the crowd one night!) We raided coffee bars, formed rescue squads for sex parties, and marched among the crowds at the dog track with Bible placards.

I still attended church, but my heart was filled with pride. Just what did these poor dead Christians know about real Christianity? I refused to listen to the wise counsel of a dear couple who loved the Lord and me and who could see that my exhausting schedule was rapidly leading me to a breakdown. They knew I was a candidate for group three, the *deranged* group. My wild career in group two finally ended after I got involved with a boy who was hiding from the police. I was trying to help him, but it was I who needed help, for the police believed I was an accessory after the fact to his many crimes.

Balance was a word I disliked; it sounded too much like compromise to me. But balance was certainly just what I needed! I needed to stop conforming to a group and start discovering and developing my own gifts.

Perhaps what I needed was a husband to help me see myself as God and others saw me. But a Christian husband seemed as impossible a dream to me as a trip to Mars! There were few Christian men in fellowships at home, and those that were there seemed weedy, weak, or insipid! It didn't seem safe to ask the Lord to provide me with a husband, for he hadn't much to choose from. I was afraid he might present me with a balding, squint-eyed spotty boy six inches shorter than me and say, "He's a great Christian; marry him!" No, it was obviously safer to forget all about marriage. I had proved over three years that God could satisfy me without a man in my life. So the obvious thing to do was head for Africa and become an intrepid missionary. There I could bury myself beneath a jungle hat and a mosquito net. With this noble intention in mind, I applied to Bible college! It was full, so they couldn't take me. I had no idea how Africa could possibly manage without me, but I decided to spend time seeking to disciple a wild group of teenagers who had found Christ through the ministry of the strange group!

I found myself with 80 teens. They were new Christians, eager to learn all I could teach them. This didn't take long, so I looked around somewhat desperately for help. All the people I asked advised me to "take them away somewhere for a retreat!" (This reminded me of the story of the feeding of the five thousand. "Send them away," the disciples pleaded. But the Lord demanded that *they* give them to eat.) Perhaps the church had nothing to give – or were they afraid of the arranged getting deranged if the strange appeared in the church pew?

So away we went to a beautiful castle, Capernwray Hall, situated at the gateway to England's Lake District. It was a Christian youth conference centre run by an organisation called Torchbearers. I hadn't known such places existed. There was freedom with discipline, fun without frivolity – balance! Here I watched the gifted staff counsel and teach, encourage and train my young people. And here it was I met a man who was to balance me!

Stuart Briscoe was tall, dark and handsome, so obviously he was a temptation sent by the devil to distract me from following the Lord! Never in those first days did it occur to me that God could give *me* a man like this. One evening while battling with my vulnerable heart, I read that Jesus sent his disciples out two by two!

"Don't tease me, Lord," I prayed. "You know my heart. You know I'm happy alone with you. So what's happening to me?" Then I read, "He who did not spare his own Son, but gave him up for us all – how will he not also, along with him, graciously give us all things?" (Romans 8:32). I knew what would happen. I'd fall in love and then God would take him away and I'd get hurt.

"If your son asks for bread, do you give him a stone? Of course not," said the Father.

"But I don't deserve him, Lord!"

"He doesn't deserve *you!*" the Lord replied. "But you surely need someone to take you in tow! Step into my plan for your life, Jill. Category four is called the *pre-arranged*. Say 'thank you,' and let's have a wedding!"

We did, and then it was I who learned that weddings last a day, but marriage is forever.

5

It Is Not Good to Live Alone

Asked to define a game of golf, a person rather cynically replied, "Golf is a good walk spoiled!" Maybe the person in question had just finished a bad round, or hadn't been trying very hard, or didn't feel it important enough to improve his game. He may have blamed the course, the equipment or his partner. If he was really upset, he might have changed clubs and partner, too!

To many people, marriage seems to be held in no higher regard than a game of golf! How sad, when marriage was intended by God to bring the greatest of human happiness. To any thinking person it is quite obvious that it's the bad golfer, not the game of golf, that's at fault. In the same way, it is not the divine institution of marriage that's at fault but the man and woman playing the course. If the rules are obeyed and the participants are willing to work at it, they might begin to enjoy their relationship.

One of the problems we face today is sheer ignorance of the rules. The biblical concept of marriage is so often untaught or is couched in church terms (such as "holy matrimony") which usually do not relate to the everyday world of the young. Before I found Christ, I thought marriage was the wedding day. Once I'd met Jesus and learned that marriage was forever, I decided I'd better find out how it worked!

Marriage, being God's idea, had to be good! Perhaps it was because marriage was his idea that he accepted in the person of Jesus Christ the invitation to the wedding at Cana in Galilee that we read about in John 2. As I wrote our wedding invitations to our relatives and friends, I sent one to heaven straight from my heart. It read, "The future Mr and Mrs D. S. Briscoe request the pleasure of the company of Jesus Christ at their wedding." I had an instant reply by air mail, "Delighted to accept!"

He was coming! How exciting! What would he do? Well – nothing – if he wasn't asked. I knew that from the Scriptures. The problem with the marriage at Cana seemed to be that he was invited as a mere guest, not as governor of the feast. The governor was the one who was in control, gave the orders and was obeyed. I didn't want Christ to be a guest on the same level as my loved ones and friends – there merely to add a bit of religion to the scene. I did not want the wine of our love to run out nor our relationship to become insipid, colourless and tasteless. I knew the secret lay in his pre-eminence as governor and our obedience to his commands. "Do whatever he tells you" (John 2:5) was the best wedding advice we'd heard anywhere. How foolish of us to buck the divine principles and do our own thing when the Bible taught that our joy (through obedience) would be better than anything we had experienced in our relationship before.

Now I discovered that the snake was still in my garden! He hadn't been absent between the end of chapter one and this point in my life; he'd just been slithering in and out and around. But never did I expect him to turn up as consistently as he did in our early days of married bliss! The snake hates any marriage that has the Lord God in control, walking and talking in the cool of the day with the two he made especially for each other and for himself. God placed man in an ideal environment, but even in Paradise something was missing. "It is not good for the man to be alone," said God (Genesis 2:18); so he set "the lonely in families" (Psalm 68:6), and he started in Eden.

The first hissing suggestion I heard from the snake, as I happily washed, cooked, worked and cared for our baby David in those early years of marriage, was the usual misquoting of Scripture for which the snake is renowned. Because it sounded familiar to me, I was taken off guard.

"It is not good for the man to be alone," he hissed in my ear. "God never intended it, so why does that Christian husband leave you alone so much? He should be here to help you with the baby and the work instead of being busy with God's business!" Next time you hear the hiss of the snake, check up on his quote. I didn't. If I had, I would have remembered that the verse about being alone referred to the man and that the woman was created to help the man, not vice versa.

The fruit of self-pity looked good to me, so I ate it. It immediately created a desire in me to encourage my husband to eat it also.

"Why don't you stay home on the weekends and evangelise here?" I asked him. "Look over there outside that Cat's Whisker coffee bar across the street. All those young people need to hear the Gospel. Why preach to a dozen little old ladies in church?"

Now let me assure you, I could not have cared less about the needy young people across the street. I was simply using them as an excuse to get my own way. I was lonely, and so I was manipulating to get Stuart to obey me rather than God. And I was using a religious excuse to accomplish my purpose. How true is the Scripture that says, "The heart is deceitful above all things and beyond cure" (Jeremiah 17:9).

Looking out of our windows and across the street, my husband commented simply, "What do you think you are here for? You reach them."

A thousand excuses leaped to my lips. "My job is to be your wife and look after you and the baby while praying and supporting your ministry. I haven't time!"

"Well, you have more time than I have," he replied. "Jill, God doesn't ask you for your husband's time, or your child's time; he asks you for your spare time!" And with this he packed his case and was gone.

"Well," said the snake, "how unfair. Anyway, you can't go over there and talk to them. They're another generation. (I was 23 years old!) Get some teens to go!" This last was said with a smug hiss, as he knew the only Christians I'd met were very young in Christ, shy and nervous. Of course he'd forgotten the principle of 1 Corinthians 1:26–28, and therefore made a bad mistake.

Seeing a way out, I accepted his advice and decided to invite three or four young people to do those things I didn't dare to do. I would stay home and pray for them (nice of me!) and make an English cup of tea (which is what you always do in times of crisis) in case they needed to retire from the battlefield to recuperate.

The Lord was about to teach me a lesson. It was the same lesson I began to learn at the beginning of this chapter. God leaned out of heaven and said to me, "Jill, you're right. It is not good for man to be alone or woman for that matter, especially if the man is called away to be about his Father's business. I'm about to rectify the matter and send you some company!" As my three brave but quaking teens went across the road to approach dozens of wild-looking youngsters outside the coffee bar, the establishment was closed because of a fight; my three well-trained evangelists panicked and invited everyone back across the street for a free cup of English tea! Looking out of what I had believed was my safe little cocoon, I discovered with horror that the time had come for me to become a butterfly!

"There you are, Jill. We brought them!" my evangelists announced triumphantly. The kids streamed into the house filling every room, chattering and kidding.

"Yes, you did!" I replied weakly. I heard the Lord chuckle. I'm sure it was the Lord. I knew it wasn't the snake, as he wasn't in the mood for laughter! Late into the night we talked and witnessed and argued and prayed. Very near midnight my husband returned from his preaching engagement, tried to get in, and couldn't! Hearing Stuart's knock, a lanky youth with hair dyed in different coloured stripes opened the door a crack and muttered, "Sorry, mate, there's no room!"

It was a new beginning for both of us. My spare time bulged with positive activity, while Stuart fought his own battles with his heart about his involvement with the teens. I sat down and made a note of my daily routine and blocked off my spare time, setting it aside for God. Young people were finding Christ, and follow-up Bible studies began in our home. I thought back to our beautiful wedding service and the text a preacher had spoken from: "It was noised abroad that Jesus was in the house." So it began to be, and the crowds came until, like the Bible story, they could hardly get near him because of the press of the crowd. I prayed, "Oh, my Lord, may your presence in our home be news around town!"

I came to realise that even though I had committed my life to Stuart, this did not mean I had committed my relationship with God to Stuart! That was still my responsibility. Even though we could read and pray and learn of him together, even though God had a special plan for our lives collectively, I needed to fulfil his plan for my life individually! I needed to guard my own personal devotional time and not let collective devotions take that place. God had work for me to do, spiritual work in areas that my husband never would have had time or talent for.

Our home could be my fishing boat during his absence. Our baby could be a means of contact among other young mothers in the park or at the store. I had a commission from God not only to care physically and practically for my family's needs in a manner that would bring glory to him, but also to bring the Gospel to every creature. I must not abdicate that responsibility just because I had got married!

So many legitimate excuses to fade off the spiritual scene were available in those happy days. As Martha, I was careful and troubled about good and necessary things, but I needed to remember Mary's better part – to sit at his feet and look in his face and listen to his word. And when I did that, I was continually reminded that two people made one must equal twice the impact for his kingdom! As God's Word says, "One [of you will] chase a thousand, or two put ten thousand to flight" (Deuteronomy 32:30).

6

The Trees of the Forest Will Clap

Six months after our ministry began among the young people outside the Cat's Whisker coffee bar, we began to experience an unsettling type of inner conviction. We felt we were being gently prepared for transfer!

Stuart was beginning to receive far more invitations for ministry than he was able to accept. His banking career offered many excellent opportunities that began to conflict with his Christian outreach, and the time had come to make a choice. Something had to go. Was it to be banking or the development of his ministry? We began to ask the Lord about it.

Guidance is a practical business. The will of God is that which lies immediately before us – the obvious, not the obscure. It had not been difficult to discern the will of God for our lives during the days that had passed. We needed to reach those lost young people on our doorstep. We didn't even need to pray about that! Prayer can be a wonderful excuse for not doing God's will. "Let's pray about it," we say, and settle for words instead of work. As God said to Joshua, "Get up off your face and go and do what I've told you to do. There is sin in the camp, and you know my principle about that. Go and put it right, and then come and pray" (Joshua 7:10–11, author's paraphrase). In the same way, we don't need to pray about whether or not we should reach the lost; the principle has already been outlined. We shouldn't pray "Shall I go?" We should pray as we go!

But now a situation arose where the next obvious thing was not quite so obvious. We had come to a crossroads, and a choice had to be made between banking or preaching. As was usual in our relationship, I arrived far too rapidly at a decision and happily said to my husband, "You pray, I'll pack!" However, as the breadwinner and head of our home, Stuart needed to be absolutely sure he was doing the right thing before he turned down an excellent offer of promotion and twelve years' service in a secure profession. So we drew up a list of the principles of guidance we found in the Scriptures. We discovered that guidance is founded on:

1. The advice of mature Christians
2. Our natural talents, abilities and spiritual gifts
3. Inner conviction as we search the Scriptures for direction, separately and together
4. Circumstances involving practical considerations having to do with money, family commitments, etc.

We then began working our way through these directives. The men Stuart sought out for counsel unanimously advised us to leave banking. Stuart's ministry had been so developed and blessed by God that these godly men felt constrained to point him toward this decision. Next we began to search the Scriptures together, reading in the book of Matthew. There we found such verses as "The harvest is plentiful but the workers are few" (Matthew 9:37), and "Do not store up for yourselves treasures on earth, where moth and rust destroy, and where thieves break in and steal" (Matthew 6:19). Very appropriate for us! Stuart travelled for the bank, and while we were miles apart one week we were amazed to be separately impressed by the same verse from the book of Isaiah which said,

You will go out in joy
and be led forth in peace;
the mountains and hills
will burst into song before you,
and all the trees of the field
will clap their hands. (Isaiah 55:12)

We had no idea why we felt so convicted that this particular verse had relevance to our situation, but we shared it and noted it down. Perhaps we would be able to understand it later. Circumstances appeared to point to full-time work as well. At exactly this point in time, two mission agencies invited us to join them without any prodding on our part. We prayed about our family commitments. To accept one of these opportunities would put us within a few miles of Stuart's recently widowed and very lonely mother. As we pondered this factor, that very morning we received a moving letter from her and our daily reading contained these words spoken by Jesus from the cross, "Behold thy mother!" (John 19:27, KJV).

As we made a list for and against all these possibilities, Stuart became convinced he had to hand in his resignation to the bank. The next decision was the hardest. Which of the two mission agencies should we choose? The lists we had made concerning both societies appeared equal, and we needed to give an answer within three short weeks. We talked and prayed and searched the Scriptures, but seemed to be no nearer to a solution. Then we asked God for a sign.

Both organisations had discussed our roles, money, and all other details; yet strangely enough, neither had mentioned accommodation.

"Let's ask the Lord to show us his will," Stuart said. "Like Gideon, we'll put out a fleece." We determined to choose whichever society offered us a house.

The night before our decision was required, the director of one of the agencies came to us and spent a wonderful evening of fellowship and prayer. We listened hard all night. There was no mention of a house! It was incredible. Every detail had been talked over. We looked at each other as we shut the door behind this good servant of the Lord. There had been no offer of a house from the alternative work either. Had we made a mistake in asking for a sign? We had to give our decision the very next day. We turned to go upstairs to bed, and suddenly the phone rang. It was the leader of one of the agencies calling to apologise for phoning at such a late hour, but telling us he had foolishly forgotten to mention a rather important detail. The detail was "the offer of a house".

We laughed for joy, we packed, and we journeyed 80 miles up the motorway to England's beautiful Lake District, where our work was to begin. We arrived late on an April evening. The next day dawned bright and clear. The birds welcomed us with triumphant song, and we walked outside and gazed around the forest of trees about to burst forth in all their spring glory. Suddenly we remembered the verse we both had discovered a few months earlier! I ran into our new home and returned with my Bible, and we read again Isaiah 55:12:

> *You will go out in joy*
> *and be led forth in peace;*
> *the mountains and hills*
> *will burst into song before you,*
> *and all the trees of the field*
> *will clap their hands.*

Guidance is easy when our will is his will. When we follow his leading, he promises we shall hear a voice behind us saying, "This is the way; walk in it" (Isaiah 30:21). When we do that, even the trees will clap their hands.

7

Triple Ripple

The novelty was wearing off. Country life was a different style of living. The peace and tranquillity of those first happy days became a somewhat oppressive silence to my city-dweller ears. Here I was, stuck in my picturesque little lodge while all the action was happening a mile away at the youth centre. I peered out of my window through the bushes, rambling roses and trees, and contemplated my mission field! All I could see were the owls, cows and blackbirds! Where were the fish?

"Start where you are with what you've got!" said the Master.

"But, Lord, haven't you forgotten something?" After all, I mused, with all he had on his mind it was perfectly conceivable that he had overlooked one or two details in my inconsequential makeup. He must have forgotten I was "good" with young people. This was obviously the area of my talent, and so he really must have made a mistake planting me among "little old ladies in rose-covered cottages." I had no knowledge or experience of old age, nor did I wish to acquire such. This area of service could well be left until I, too, was 70 years old and lived in similar rose-covered quarters!

I was, of course, making the common mistake of telling God how I would serve him and who I would reach for him. I watched the little river bubbling over the rocks under the beautiful stone bridge near our house and threw pebbles moodily into the pool beneath me. As I watched the ripples, they seemed to echo the verse, "You will be my witnesses in Jerusalem, and in all Judea and Samaria, and to the ends of the earth" (Acts 1:8). The Lord seemed to be saying to me, "Start where you are with what you've got (Jerusalem), the circle will widen (Judea), I'll lead you to people you don't particularly like to tell them of me (Samaria), and unto the uttermost parts of the earth."

Reluctantly I gave in. The next day, while wheeling our baby Peter in his carriage and clutching the sticky hand of four-year-old David, I began my intrepid spy work. I felt like Caleb sneaking into the Promised Land. However, I found that my giants were hardly as imposing or frightening as his. I nodded cheerfully to Mrs T. in her English garden, chatted to Mrs S. as she rocked on her porch, and at last plucked up courage to knock on a few doors and invite the women to my cottage to read the Bible. They were all very polite and said "Yes, thank you" they would be pleased to come.

I waited expectantly. It was a long wait because no one came. Disappointed, I tried to refrain from saying, "I told you so!" to the Lord and went to gently inquire of the ladies why they had not been able to come. They appeared embarrassed and offered varied excuses. I smiled cheerfully and reissued my invitations. They assured me they would be there next time. They weren't!

Well now, there was my responsibility over with. Surely I couldn't impose on their kindness any more! Shortly after these fruitless efforts on my behalf, a teenage boy who had recently come to Christ became concerned about his grandmother and invited me to attend the "old age pensioners" meeting (like a senior-citizens group) with him and his grandmother. I went grudgingly. I was still sure I knew far better than God how I should be used. I looked around the room. All the men and women there were over 65 years of age, as this was the qualifying age to join this excellent group. They were sweet, but I was bored. I must say, however, that I certainly was convicted by my young friend's obvious love and concern for these older people. The meeting began, and suddenly I was riveted to my seat.

"We will begin," said the chairman, "by reading out the death roll from last month," which he proceeded to do. As we all stood in remembrance of these souls who had gone forth into eternity, my young friend dug me in the ribs.

"See what I mean?" he hissed. "These people need Christ now!"

I was convinced and ashamed! The next day found me knocking at doors for a third time. A few promised to come, and this time they kept their word. One woman was lame, one could not see, one was hard of hearing, and all were over 65. The pebble dropped. Suddenly I found that I was surrounded by mothers and grandmothers, love and encouragement, wisdom and gentleness. I had no idea Jerusalem was so inundated with older people. We sang, we prayed, we read the Scriptures, and our numbers grew week by week. When the time came for our special Christmas meeting, we had to remove all the furniture and place it in the garage. Forty ladies gathered, and at the end of the service Stuart presented a homemade cake to the oldest one present! He had all of the women stand up while we counted upwards from 65. At last one little lady was left standing alone, beaming with pride. But she looked very surprised to receive the cake that Stuart happily handed to her. Then I told her she could sit down. There was no response. And someone informed me she wasn't the oldest at all. She was just deaf!

The ripples widened, the women's daughters began to attend the meetings, and we moved out of our little lodge into larger accommodation. I couldn't believe the love that was shed abroad in my heart by the Holy Spirit for this group of people. Starting where I was with what I had brought me a discovery of abilities that I had no idea I possessed. One day some of the daughters brought along their teenage daughters, and my heart leaped for joy. The triple ripple! I understood the principle at last. What a perfectly natural sequence of events, and what a divine way to reach the young people – through grandmother praying and mother finding Christ.

"Now," said the Master, "we'll start to use all that talent you were boasting about!" Subdued, I wondered whether I was cut out for teen work after all. "You don't know your gifts unless you try to exercise them," said the Master. "Never decide where you should be used again. That's my business. Having started where you are with what you've got, let's just see where the ripple will lead you!"

8

The Barn

Some people are always looking for a new interest or hobby. New pursuits are the spice of life for them. My Bible suggested a new pursuit to me. I read in Romans 12:13 that I should "practise hospitality". Apparently the word *practise* meant to pursue. In Acts 16:14 Lydia opened her heart to Christ, and one verse later she was busy opening her home and pursuing Paul, Silas and their friends to persuade them to stay with her. An open heart ought to mean an open home. I had let the Lord in when he knocked on the door of my life; when, then, did I find myself denying other people entry?

"Some teens are so easy to love, and others I don't even like!" I complained to the Lord.

"I loved you when there was nothing lovely to love!" he rejoined. "While you were yet a sinner I died for you" (Romans 5:8, author's paraphrase).

"But don't I have a 'right' to invite whom I want into my own home?" I questioned.

"Your home?" my heavenly landlord inquired patiently. "Don't you remember you signed it over to me, and isn't it lawful for me to do what I will with my own?" We had been through all that before, so I hurriedly agreed.

"Since this is my house," he continued, "don't you think it is reasonable for me to invite whom I will into it?" Next he pointed to my locked and shuttered heart that was so afraid of opening up and getting hurt, and he commented, "Remember, this is my heart, too. Why don't you undo the locks and let me in?"

"Oh, Lord, you are in. Don't you remember I gave you free entry years ago!" (As if he suffered from amnesia!)

"As much as you do it unto the least of these my brethren, you do it unto me!" the owner of my property reminded me.

Just then the doorbell rang, and three members of our group who had been cycling by stopped in to see me.

There was a snake in my kitchen. He slithered around drawing my attention to many good reasons why this particular evening was not a convenient time to entertain: the pile of washing to be done, the half-finished letter to my husband, a baby's cry upstairs. I kicked at him (the snake, not the baby), missed him, but managed to tell him before he disappeared that I'd decided from now on to try and live a "plan-less" life like the Lord Jesus had lived. My schedule would from henceforth be set in heaven. I decided to stop minding God's business for him. His was the responsibility; he could do the worrying!

"Come in," I said, grabbing the three youths and yanking them inside. "Oh, do come in. Thank you so much for coming!"

Rather surprised at the warmth of my welcome, they hesitantly entered my home and, though they didn't know it then, my heart. The harvest stands ready, but how hard are the hearts of the harvesters! The fear of the cost of involvement is so great, and often the heavenly farmer finds nowhere to stack his grain.

The harvest was truly ready in our small corner of the mission field. The labourers were few but fervent! Most nights of the week newly gathered sheaves began to be untidily piled around our house. Our little abode was used, but not abused. A small sign reading, "Where do you think you are going?" was usually enough to restrict movement from private areas of the house. We sang, we shared, we prayed, we opened the Bible and studied it verse by verse. We sought out the meaning, put it into our own words, and applied it to our lives and circumstances. It was piercingly relevant. Day after day, week after week, the young people came, bringing their friends (and enemies) with them. From that time forward it was a question of committing the day to him and accepting whatever happened as coming from him.

There came a time, however, when "no more sheaves could be safely gathered in!" We were not in a position to "pull down our barns and build greater," and we prayed to the Lord for an answer to our predicament.

A young mother had been coming to the Bible study for many weeks. She was shy and sweet and needed a ride to the meetings. Each time I drove her home, I would pray, "Lord, don't let me rush her into making a decision; help me to give her plenty of time to understand."

One day she said to me in exasperation, "Jill, when are you going to help me find Christ? I'd been praying ever since that very first study time that you would have the courage to speak to me!"

With help, she ushered Christ in with her tears. The very next week her husband accepted the Lord, and together they invited us to use their barn, where their cattle were wintered, for our meetings.

The sheaves were absolutely delighted! Two thousand years ago Christ had been born in a stable. It was obviously the sort of place he delighted to visit, and in the months ahead he was to be born again in many a teenage heart. The premises were old and needed plenty of work. The temptation was to call a work party of worthy willing workers (adults preferably), roll up our sleeves, and do the work. Yet I felt it would be better to let the teens fix it up for themselves. We gave them responsibility (before they showed any), letting them splash paint merrily over everything in sight (it could always be mopped up when they had all gone happily home), and just made sure they knew it belonged to "them". The value of the united project was immense.

One elementary need, that of transportation, was wonderfully taken care of. A missionary, hearing of our lack of a vehicle, signed his mini-bus over to us. For years it "flew" mile after mile collecting and depositing excited teens. Sometimes it ran more on prayer than petrol, but God always provided just enough money for our needs, though never enough to stop us from being dependent on the giver of our gifts. One day we had a blowout. We got the car to a garage to repair the tyre, but we never replaced the spare. Whether we couldn't afford to replace it or we simply forgot about it, I cannot recall. But for years the bus served us well, covering hundreds of miles over rough roads, carrying gangs of young people to share their faith in Christ without another flat tyre. The next blowout we had was the week after we traded in our old exhausted chariot for a new one. The new vehicle was, of course, accompanied by that saving spare wheel!

Leaders emerged as responsibility and authority were given to them. They were usually as surprised as we were by their accomplishments and began to spearhead new avenues of outreach.

"How would you like to captain a Christian football team?" we asked a fine boy who loved the Lord, football and teaching little boys – in that order!

"Oh, I couldn't do that!" he protested.

"How do you know, if you have never tried?" we inquired.

Accepting the challenge, he soon had his team playing other local clubs. He would then invite the visitors back to the barn where they would eat and have a time of sharing. Junior teams sprang up, and boys between the ages of eight and twelve began to come around. We lovingly called this group "the beasties". If you have little boys between these ages, you might know why we named them that! Individually they were great; collectively they were "the beasties".

God gave me a special helper and friend who had a patient and understanding love for this particular group. These boys drove everyone else to distraction, but Angela heeded our senior missionary's comment that "boys will be boys but one day they will be men," and she gave herself unstintingly to the children.

Angela said, "If we can touch base with this gang now, even if it seems impossible to teach them spiritual realities at the moment, I believe we'll reach half of them by the time they're sixteen. If we wait till they're grown, we'll win only two or three of them!" She was to be proven absolutely right.

Despite the successes, the work lacked a vision. I learned that youth work needs to begin when the "youth" are five or six years old! We discovered that children's Bible clubs could be set up on school premises. Yet this needed lots of faith, much prayer, and a bold approach. For example: "Please, 'Mr Headmaster', we have seven or eight teenagers who want to give their spare time to influence these little ones for God and teach them the Bible. This, of course, will make them better pupils and will also make you a mighty popular man among pleased parents! Will you help us?" Having said this, we took a deep breath, sent a telegram prayer, and tried to maintain a weak smile!

What relief and praise followed as "Mr Headmaster" smiled and said, "Certainly. Use what you will. It' a nice change to see teenagers doing something worthwhile."

Soon we had six clubs led by teens in different locations throughout the town. "Train up a child in the way he should go," says the Scripture. "And walk there yourself once in a while," added a shrewd thinker. Our teachers discovered that they needed to watch their behaviour and attend to their lives. Leadership required a certain standard of behaviour, a lot of growing up, plenty of discipline and much study. What a wonderful way to keep teenagers occupied – seeking to be like

Christ and sharing his life with others. Many a time a boy or girl would come to us and say, "Since I've become a Christian I've had to stop going to the places I used to go, so what do I do with all this free time I have on my hands?" Now we had opportunities of service for them, and we found out through this experience that entertaining newly converted teenagers was *not* the way to keep them. "Employing" them was!

While all the children's work was developing, other teens were setting off to their old haunts to bring their friends to meet Jesus. We called this effort to reach their friends Operation Andrew because Andrew had brought his brother to the Lord. It was soon in full swing. When they couldn't persuade their friends to leave the pub, coffee bar, discotheque or dance hall, they began to call me and say, "Please come to us, Jill. They're asking questions we can't answer. They are interested but are afraid to come up to the barn." Immediately the snake flashed a picture in front of me. I saw myself slinking quietly into the entrance of the pub while at the bus stop opposite stood the minister from my church and the local church gossiper!

"What about your reputation?" the snake hissed. "What will people think?" (As if he cared anyway!)

I made an excuse to the boy on the telephone and hung up. Wrestling all evening with my pride, I busily wasted time. I knew I mustn't read the Bible. I'd be confronted with the answer! By bedtime, however, I was "willing to be made willing", which is the first step to obedience! I opened the Bible and was not a bit surprised to read that he "made himself nothing" (Philippians 2:7). The next night, head high, I walked into the bar, sat down with the boys, and found needy, interested souls ready to be reached. Why did I have to learn the same things over and over again? It was the triple ripple lesson – the widening impact, the reaching out to Samaritans. These were the despised young people that many respectable "religious" folk at Jerusalem wouldn't have anything to do with!

The success of the visit gave me an idea. If the young people in this bar were as interested and open as this, what about the myriad other establishments in the area? "The best way to begin is to begin," said R. A. Torrey. (There are some things you don't even need to pray about! Remember?) Systematically we began to visit each bar in our area. We were always careful to ask permission from the manager. After explaining what was involved, we were never refused entry. We sang, testified or spoke for a few minutes, then gave out Bibles and Christian literature and spent time chatting with people. And always we were invited back again. I felt this wasn't particularly a compliment to us, as I could see that these men hadn't the slightest conception of how Christ could change someone and fill his life so completely that he would no longer need to be drunk with wine. If they had realised this, I'm sure they wouldn't have let us in to threaten their business!

Invariably, as we entered a bar, something always happened which really sickened me. As we grouped around the piano to sing spirituals or favourite hymns, the patrons' hands would go into their pockets to fish out some money. What a sad picture they had of Christ's glorious church. Their actions said more clearly than words, "Here comes the church begging as usual!"

Getting upset, I would raise my voice and say something like, "Folks, please, we don't want your money. We haven't come to ask for something; we've come to give you someone. We are wealthy beyond measure because we have Christ, and he is all we need!" This usually got everyone's attention, and we were in for a great evening of sharing.

It soon became apparent that we needed to get organised. Buying a map of the district, we spent one whole evening spying out the land. We marked the bars, restaurants, coffee bars, discos and open-air places where young people congregated. Then we planned a systematic blitz on each place in turn. One week it would be street work, the next coffee bars, after that pubs, and then the fairgrounds and amusement arcades.

We began to learn that different types of "bait" were needed to catch different types of fish. Music was a great attention-getter in some places; testimonies, skits or five-minute sermons in others; and in some the need for dramatic presentation became apparent. Therefore, we wrote a musical play called *Sitting on the Fence*. It was a simple story of a young girl sitting on a wooden fence with the devil on one side and the preacher on the other. The music and the story told of the fight for her soul. We took this simple dramatisation to shopping centres, coffee bars and any other place that would have us. It became a real weapon for the Lord and is still being used today in many parts of the world. I discovered that drama could be a real entrance into places that wouldn't let us in "just to preach".

Many times we received a rough reception, but the teens were simply exhilarated with the privilege of suffering for his sake! They were far more courageous than I. Many a time I would be busy exhorting them in prayer to be brave and to fight the foe – with bowed head and knocking knees! When I opened my eyes, I would find myself alone. The army was already engaged in the conflict, while I was still trying to get into my armour!

On one such night, after having launched the team into their evangelistic work, I found myself without a goal for the evening. I wandered toward a huge dance hall into which dozens of teens were streaming and out of which deafening music emanated. I began to pray. (Not very hard, in case he heard me and told me to be the answer to my own prayer!) "Oh, Lord," I intoned, "give me the courage to go inside!" I neither expected it nor wanted it. When the courage didn't arrive, I heaved a sigh of relief and returned home to pray for the poor people in that den of iniquity. That night I "happened" to be reading the Book of Romans where Paul is being pretty logical in explaining the way the Gospel must be physically taken to the people who have never heard. "Everyone who calls on the name of the Lord will be saved. How, then, can they call on the one they have not believed in? And how can they believe in the one of whom they have not heard? And how can they hear without someone preaching to them? And how can they preach unless they are sent?" (Romans 10:13–15)

"Well, I wasn't sent," I concluded. At once I remembered a sermon preached by my own husband on this very passage. Regarding this point he had said, "Some went and were never sent, some were sent and never went, some were sent and went!"

"I sent you," said the Lord. "You received your commission when I told you to go into all the world and preach the Gospel to every creature. That dance hall is the bit of the world to which I'm sending you."

The next week found me back at the scene of my defeat. I was disappointed when I discovered I felt just the same. Standing outside the dance hall all evening, I prayed. And this time I really meant it! But still the courage didn't come, and I retired home beaten again. Returning to the scene of the battle the following week, I began my usual demands for courage to do his will. Suddenly I realised something absolutely elementary. The courage might never come! Whether it did or not was totally irrelevant. I needed to obey. I needed to go in without the courage. It was a matter of my will and intellect motivating me to obedience. So often my obedience had depended upon my feelings. If I felt like it, I would obey. If I didn't, I wouldn't! And so I applied my will to my feet (which I suddenly noticed had a snake wrapped firmly around them). "Feet, move!" I said. They did. The snake, who cannot wrap up the feet of obedience, hurriedly unwound from my ankles. I found myself inside the dance hall where the courage was waiting for me!

"Take me to the manager," a voice demanded. I looked around to see who had followed me inside. There was no one there. It was *I* who had demanded the interview! Once in the man's office, perfectly calm and collected, I heard myself asking if I might speak to the thousand teenagers gyrating to the unbelievably loud rock music. After answering many questions and sharing Christ with the manager, an open door was set in front of me that no one could shut (Revelation 3:8). Surely God gave me favour in the man's sight.

Week after week, young people found Christ in that place, and today they are in the vanguard of youth work. And I learned one of the most valuable lessons of my Christian life: To obey, without stipulating conditions, is what being a soldier for Jesus Christ is all about!

9

Mary's Little Box

Days passed into months and months into years. Stuart's ministry developed and took him away for increasing amounts of time. Having once dealt with my resentful heart about the issue of his absence, I didn't expect to have to deal with it again. I learned the hard way. Victory won yesterday does not mean victory automatically dispensed for the rest of life.

Although I kept myself thoroughly involved and saw much blessing, once more I began to fall prey to discontentment and self-pity. I read the story of Mary's little alabaster box of ointment. I believe Jewish girls kept these treasured boxes of ointment as security. They were their "marriage boxes". If they never married, the precious ointment would provide for them. If they did marry, the proceeds would be part of their parental provision. They were, as the Bible says, "very precious". So was mine!

My "marriage box" again became more valuable than my relationship with my Lord and Saviour Jesus Christ. I was amazed at how hypocritical I could be, pretending all was well yet knowing differently. I watched my senior missionaries and tried to copy their ways. I learned to wave my husband off on a three-month tour with just the right evangelical smile. With a false earnestness which apparently was believed, I mouthed the usual pious platitudes to those who sympathised over our separation. "Oh, the Lord will look after us. Don't worry. He will give us the peace we need and make it all up to us in some way," I assured them. Now this was true and I knew it, but I was frosting up solidly on the inside. The warmth of the Lord's provision was far from my experience. The problem was that I didn't want this help. I wanted my husband!

I stopped reading the Bible (it was far too relevant), and I stopped praying. After all, I had nothing to say and certainly didn't want to hear his voice any more. Why, the last time I'd turned to the Word for comfort, my eyes had been drawn to the words, "Is it not lawful for me to do what I will with mine own?"

"It may be 'lawful'," I snapped, shutting my Bible, "but I think it is awful!"

At this point in my spiritual experience I hadn't learned that his rod and staff comfort the stupid wayward sheep. I didn't like the prods one little bit, nor did I appreciate his staff reaching down into my hole of depression to get me out. Depression suited me much better. The snake slithered in beside me, and we spent a few dreadful weeks hissing out our mistrust of God's ways.

"Don't give in," the snake advised. "If you do, you know he won't let Stuart stay at home; he'll just take Stuart away all the more! Stand up for your rights! Let your husband know how unhappy you are. You know how to do that, don't you? When he says, 'Is anything wrong, dear?' say 'No, nothing' in such a way that he knows perfectly well there is!"

I knew exactly what he was talking about and knew how well I could do just that. I was appalled as I realised the power I had as a Christian wife. I could so easily make my husband worry about me. I could hinder or even prevent him from obeying God! Standing up for my rights couldn't mean that! The snake had overstepped himself again, and I suddenly recognised the source of my thoughts. I began to open up the lines of communication with God again.

"You don't know what it is like being so lonely, Lord," I accused him.

"My Son left him for 30 years one time!" he replied.

"Well," I countered, "you don't know what it is like to be separated. You were with him in spirit." The shadow of the cross and the voice of one crying, "My God, My God, Why hast thou forsaken me?" was his answer.

"It was your sin, all that rebellion and self-pity and anger, that separated me from my Son, Jill. I punished him instead of you because I love you, and it's because I love you that I want you to believe that! My will for your life is good and perfect and *acceptable*."

My disobedience had so numbed my feelings that my heart couldn't believe that his will could be acceptable. Endurable, yes, but not acceptable! However, I could apply my mind and my will to respond. I needed to start reading the Bible again even though I knew I would read things that would convict and condemn me.

I began where I had left off – the story of Mary's little box. I fought a battle with my pride. I knew I should go and seek counsel from my senior missionary. She was one who had obviously yielded her marriage box years before and apparently was enjoying happiness and victory.

The snake's tail twitched in horror. "Just imagine her face," he shrieked. "How can you bear to let her know you are a failure? Keep up appearances. Nobody needs to know your heart's condition!" I thought of Mary. How hard it must have been for her to bring her "marriage box" out in front of all those people and give it to Jesus. Everyone knew the disciples had left all to follow him, and here she was with an unyielded box! What would they say? It would be much better to keep it hidden. She knew Jesus would never take it from her by force. Surely it was enough to sit at his feet, listen to his word, entertain him in her home, and keep her little box hidden and intact.

At last I went and talked with the senior missionary. I discovered the breakage of her little alabaster box had been as difficult in her experience as mine. She was loving and sympathetic but very firm with me.

"Jill, you've given him everything except this one little box; and it doesn't matter whether it's a marriage box or a box of another sort, holding back anything is backsliding. You'll never move one step forward, never hear his Word in your heart, never see an answer to prayer, when there is known disobedience in your life!"

I thought again of Achan's sin in the Old Testament (Joshua 7:18–26). Buried deep within his tent was the treasure Achan thought no one knew about! But God knew. No depth of earth can hide the precious things we seek to conceal in disobedience. They only spoil, hidden within the cold earth. I, like Achan, knew my disobedience would bring trouble to my loved ones and to God's people. No more victories could be won until all had been exposed. How grateful I was that I didn't live in Old Testament times. If I had, I suppose I would have been stoned to death many times over by now!

I read Mark 14 over and over. "Lord, I can't give it to you. It's too precious. I'll never be like Mary; but if you will make me 'un-me-like' and work the miracle in my heart, I will give you permission to take it from me. I'm through struggling. I've had enough," I prayed. He changed my attitude, and the box was gone. The aroma of the ointment filled the house and the sweet fragrance of life attracted many people to the Saviour.

But some disciples responded as they had in the Gospel story by telling me it was a waste. "God doesn't intend you to have a separated marriage! It could have been used some other way."

But I didn't listen. Washing his feet with my tears, I spilled ointment and prayed, "Oh, God, stop me from trying to scrape this up and put it back in the box again!"

"People will come to know about me because of the aroma," God replied.

A miracle had happened in my heart. My situation was acceptable! I was at peace.

10

The Warehouse

hat we need now," an excited teenager commented, "is a big old warehouse!" I observed him with a certain measure of resentment.

"You need to learn to be content with what you have!" I retorted.

"Typical teenager," the snake agreed. "They are never satisfied. You're quite right to be irritated. I think you're doing quite enough. Anyway, don't you think you need to consolidate?"

"Solidate" was what he meant. Set my feet in concrete was what he'd like! As far as the snake and his devices were concerned, all progress must be impeded at all cost! Late that evening, seeking to dismiss the teenager's bright-eyed excitement from my mind's eye, I buried my head in the Bible. I read the exhortation in Luke 17:7–10 about the servant who had done those things which were simply his duty. I read that having done all, he was to consider himself an unprofitable servant. Well, I thought, that's a bit tough. It couldn't be referring to me. I thought proudly of all the bare harvest fields around. Surely he expected other farmers to do their share. It would be quite wrong to trespass on their property. Arriving at this smug decision, I was further irritated to be confronted again by the same waving young sheaf, demanding a warehouse to be stacked in!

"I found it," he shouted exuberantly. "A huge old warehouse. It used to store grain, and it's been empty for years and years. It's so big, four stories high, and it stretches a whole block. I've been through it, too; there are old stone walls, wooden beams everywhere, crooked old chimneys and wobbly floors. There's a couple of dead rats in the basement and a bit of smelly water, but it won't take much to clear that up!"

That did it; the rats, I mean! I appealed to the snake for help. He provided me with immediate, out-of-context Scriptures.

"Try 'Come apart and rest awhile'," he suggested. "Or what about, 'So he gives his beloved sheep'?"

"Just come down and look at it," the excited sheaf pleaded. "That's all I'm asking you to do."

And so I did, and one look was enough. The whole scene spelled "work" which I didn't like, "money" which we didn't have, and "time" which I wouldn't take. I promised the sheaf I'd pray about it, which was a great excuse for not getting involved.

A few days later an incident occurred which pointed to the glaring need for a new headquarters. I reluctantly turned to the "Word" for direction. I decided that if I found "anything" that directly referred to a warehouse then I would be willing to investigate the whole thing. Of course my attitude was completely wrong.

Unlike Gideon, who put his fleece out overnight knowing God could use the morning dew to show him the way, I decided to put mine out at midday when I was pretty certain there wouldn't be any dew around! I was going to search for my answer in a limited area of the Bible, thereby making it pretty hard for the Lord.

How foolish we mortals are. As if God cannot produce dew at midday if he wishes! Well, he produced a warehouse in the book of Malachi for me! Choosing in my ignorance an obscure portion of the Scriptures, presuming myself perfectly safe, I began to read. The snake, who apparently hadn't read Malachi either, curled up and went to sleep! I scanned chapter 1, relaxed in chapter 2, and let out a scream when I arrived at chapter 3, verse 10, which read, "'Bring the whole tithe into the storehouse, that there may be food in my house. Test me in this,' says the LORD Almighty, 'and see if I will not throw open the floodgates of heaven and pour out so much blessing that you will not have room enough for it.'" The scream woke the snake and my baby.

"I'm warning you," the snake screamed. "Snakes love warehouses, and if you dare buy it, I'll have a snake hanging from every beam!"

I told him to get lost. How could I ignore such an extraordinary verse of Scripture! I read the verse again, carefully and with a certain fearfulness, yet with a great new desire born within me by the Spirit of God to listen to his instructions and obey his Word! "Bring ye all," said the Lord. "That's the first thing. Prove me now; that's the next thing. Exercise faith to claim my promise that I'll open the windows of heaven, and there will not be room to receive the blessing." With the eyes of faith I saw in that moment a full warehouse. I heard the happy songs of the harvesters, saw the Lord of the harvest receiving honour and glory from the watchers, and I asked him to forgive my fleshly reticence. I didn't have any idea how I was physically going to do more than I was doing, but I knew I had to try.

It's all very well to have visions in the night, to weep in acquiescing prayer, to claim the promises of God, but the time comes to get up and go! I had to become part of the answer to my prayer. So it was for Jonah. One day this bigoted, fervent Jew was praying to Jehovah. He was begging the Lord to do something with the aggressive Ninevites! God told him to go and be the answer to his own prayer. So he got up and ran – in the opposite direction! God brought him back by special submarine, and he then grudgingly began to preach the message God had given him. Starting on one side of the city, he preached his way straight through and walked out the other side. He then sat down to watch God work!

How often I was wont to do the same thing. This was all the wrong way around. God had sat down and rested after his work of creation was finished; Christ had sat down at his right hand after our redemption was accomplished; now "they" wanted to watch "me" work. It was my turn!

It would have been a simple matter to walk through the warehouse and out the other side, build my booth of observation, and sit down to watch the kids roll up their sleeves and get down to it. Jesus had chosen to show me a better way. The Gospel narrative showed him walking through the Ninevehs of this world preaching repentance. He had not passed through and then sat down in an observation booth in the heavenlies to watch God avenge himself on our sin. He had lingered in the city to be the answer to our need. His were the hands that touched the dirty lepers. His were the hardened carpenter's muscles working for 30 years to provide for a widowed mother and her family. He hadn't walked past the cross to sit in judgement and watch us hang there seeking to atone for our sin! He had been crucified to become the answer to his own prayer for us!

Too often I hear people say they are not led of the Spirit to do a certain job. Often this is nothing more than a pious platitude to cover our unsoiled, worthless hands. I knew in that moment of time that one day when I stood before my Lord he would gently take my hands and turn them over looking for the callouses!

The Lord had wonderfully arranged my home affairs to give me time for this venture. At the beginning of the work my little ones were in bed at 6.00 pm, and I could be out at night when they retired, leaving them in the care of a baby-sitter. Now they were growing up and at school and I could be absent during the day. This way I was home when they were. What great opportunities now availed themselves to me to share Christ and give encouragement to the young people during many practical work parties. Working shoulder to shoulder with the teens, getting down in the unbelievable muck of a stagnant flooded cellar, and heaving bucket loads of slime up a rickety ladder brought a real sticky comradeship! It was activity not for the sake of activity, but with an object in view.

We certainly had our difficulties! One of my mistakes was made when we needed to lay a new concrete floor in the cellar. I had been advised to use a certain brand of concrete and promptly ordered one ton of "ready-mix" to be delivered to the warehouse at 4.00 pm. I instructed the man to deliver it onto the pavement outside the warehouse. Three times he asked me, "What exact time will you need it?" I wondered why he had this peculiar fixation about time; however, I repeated my instructions to dump it outside the entrance at 4.00 pm. As I approached the building at 8.00 pm that night to prepare for the work party, I wondered where they had put the bags of concrete mix. I also wondered why I had never noticed that huge mountain on the pavement outside our building! It was then I realised that instead of receiving bags for "ready-mix" concrete, I had received one ton of already mixed (and already set) concrete!

Frantically I rang the youth centre for help. The men left the meeting immediately and ran to aid us with axes, picks, shovels and buckets! They cut through the four-inch-thick crust, filled their buckets with the crumbly, heavy concrete, and, making a human chain, passed the whole ton down a rickety ladder into the cellar. About 11.00 pm I heard my husband's voice asking ominously, "Has anybody seen Jill?" No one had because I was hiding in a corner in the basement!

Despite my mistakes the warehouse was soon in use. It became obvious that God was busy instructing his angels to open his heavenly floodgates of blessing. I thought back to my promise verse, "Bring the whole tithe into the storehouse," and wondered if I had fulfilled the conditions of blessings. The whole tithe. Well, I'd surely brought in lots of physical hard work, but what about talent?

The snake and I had been reading the advertisements in the local newspaper. He had been suggesting that I go back to teaching to have some extra spending money. Not that extra spending money was wrong. It was just that the snake knew the Lord of the harvest house was planning on my fulfilling all the conditions, while he was trying to sidetrack me.

"Bring your trained talent into the warehouse, Jill," the Lord instructed me. "Start a nursery school; teach for me."

"What a ridiculous idea," the snake protested. "What health authority would give you permission for a nursery school in this dirty place?"

I was inclined to agree, especially since I didn't particularly like the idea of working for nothing! The Lord took me back in memory to our daughter's beautiful dedication service. As I had held her in my arms, the preacher had given Stuart and me a text: "Take this child and nurse it for me and I will give thee thy wages." I thought of the hundreds of little children being offered to me with these same words.

"I will give you your wages, Jill; work for me," said the Lord.

So we buried the snake underneath the pile of newspaper advertisements and made a nursery school on the first floor of the building. The income from this venture finally provided wages for full-time staff for the youth work. The windows opened wider. We began to reach many families in the district. Each day in the nursery school we would have a half-hour of Bible study time and the children would take the things they had learned home to their parents. Soon the mothers and fathers came to us asking for children's Bibles so that they might help tell their children about God.

By now the work was expanding in all directions. Days hurried by – full, happy, hard-working days. Baby sheaves in the morning, big ones in the evening. The Bible is so full of promises to claim, I thought. "Teach me, O Lord," I prayed, "if the floodgates of heaven aren't open and my warehouse is empty, it's simply because I'm not fulfilling the conditions."

11

It's All Right for Abraham

ave you a "besetting sin" – one area of weakness in your life that is weak forever? We all seem to. I thought about Moses. He had a fiery temper. He demonstrated it from his watery coffin by screaming in baby tantrums at the crocodiles. It manifested itself in cold-blooded fury when, after carefully "looking this way and that way", he murdered the Egyptian who was tormenting his Hebrew brother. He proved its dominion over him when he descended down the mountain having seen God face to face. Finding the naked, idolatrous worshippers, he lost his cool completely by literally breaking the Ten Commandments! Was it desperation or temper that caused him to sin by smiting the rock twice? Yes, it certainly appeared that Moses had a besetting sin.

The snake plays on our weaknesses. He is not a gentleman! He delights in kicking us when we are down and is neither sorry nor sympathetic. He hates us. He would destroy us if he could; and because he can't, he would render us desperate and inoperative by continually attacking our main area of weakness. At times being aware of his devices doesn't even help. We can be fully aware of what he is doing; but after saying "no" for weeks, months, or even years, there can come a time when we say "yes". Perhaps we are lax in our relationship with God or lazy in our service. Maybe we are like David who was caught "looking" and forgot to bring "every thought" into captivity to Christ.

There came a time after the initial establishing of the warehouse that I found myself tired out physically and somewhat depressed. Metaphorically speaking, I was like David. At a time when kings should have been going forth to battle, I was staying at home. As an old Chinese proverb says, "You can't stop the birds from flying over your head, but you can stop them from nesting in your hair!" That's true. The eggs were laid, and the young were hatched in my hair before I lifted a finger to do anything about it!

It happened at a meeting of all places. There I was, sitting on the front row in a packed room listening to my husband preaching a most powerful message on Abraham. Suddenly without any warning the snake, who was sitting beside me (I noticed his Bible was upside down), said, "Have you forgotten he's going away tomorrow for three months? You should be at home packing, comforting your poor children, and praying for yourself!" I tried to ignore him. After all, Stuart's voice was loud enough to drown him out. But he entangled himself around my Bible and tried to distract me. What was he doing? Well, he was actually preaching his own sermon from my husband's text! I couldn't believe that two such contrasting messages could come from the same source. As Stuart preached his heart out to hundreds of attentive teens, the snake was preaching one of his own messages right in my ear!

He was saying to me, "It's all right for Abraham. He was just like your husband. Look at him up there, all that faith oozing out. He's going off tomorrow to a land he 'knows not of' and will no doubt do great exploits for God. But what about Isaac? That's you!"

As soon as I began to give my full attention to the snake's interpretation of the passage, I was in trouble. I shut off the preacher and turned on the snake! And I did it all "behind the smile"!

As I walked home I began voluntarily to wallow in a sea of self-pity. The snake was right. What about poor old Isaac? It was all right for Abraham, but it was Isaac who was bound upon the altar and would feel the knife! The same old struggle began; the snake was attacking the same old weak spot. The future, husbandless and lonely, stretched before me. My frustration grew. This had been yielded before. If the Bible said I was dead to sin, why was I leaping off the altar of sacrifice at this moment of time and feeling very much alive?

This was to be Stuart's last night at home before a journey that would take him to the primitive mission fields of the world. There he would help to minister to hundreds of missionaries who were tired and dry, having had no opportunity for spiritual food for months, perhaps even years. I thought about Isaac and how he had managed to acquiesce to God's plan for his life: He must have chosen to die. He was not a little boy, but in all probability a grown teenager. He must have submitted himself trustingly to his father's will, no matter how fearful he was. He must have believed they would both "come again" to the men who were waiting a little way off. In other words, he believed that life would come through death!

This was my choice. I had to get back on that altar and stay there. By the time Stuart returned, weary and ready to pack his bag and get to sleep, the battle was won. I handed my husband the poem I had written that clearly explained my inner struggle; then I printed the last verse in large letters at the front of my Bible.

An Isaac experience

It's all right for Abraham;
God counts him as his friend.
Whilst I must be his enemy
Whose life he longs to end.
It's all right for Abraham,
Experienced in the art
Of glad obedience when it means
A dagger through my heart.

My father bound me hand and foot
And laid me on the pyre.
I wondered why God hated me
To torture me with fire.
I must be very wicked
Or have ceased to play my part;
I'd know in just a minute
When the knife plunged through my heart.

But greater than my fear of death,
My heart at Abraham's aim;
His love for God transcended
The love for me he'd claimed.
Then God revealed the truth to me –
My pride *had felt the knife;*
That's why there was an altar,
The ropes, the fire – my life.

When you're bound upon the altar
By the hands of those you love,
You don't know there'll be deliverance
By the voice of God above.
Then **that's** *the time to* **trust the Man**
Whom God counts as his friend;
The faith of him who puts God first
Will save you in the end.

It's **not** *all right for Abraham,*
Young Isaac learned that day;
He watched his inward agony,
With groans he heard him pray.
And suddenly he longed to help
And cried in glad submission,
"Dear Father, sacrifice your son;
You have my full permission!"

It's all right for Isaac now –
It's all right to die.
'Cause if I die, I do believe
A resurrection I'll achieve.
I really feel quite lyrical;
I'm going to be a miracle!

I didn't know it then, but this was to be the last long period of separation for us for a while. I'm so glad I made it back to the altar.

My days were busy and exciting, fuller than they had ever been. It was summertime, and open-air meetings were being held at a nearby seaside town. A few churches in the town got together and asked me to bring a team of young people to lead a service for them.

The organisers had set up the meeting in a huge parking lot. At one end about 100 boys on their motor-bikes stood talking together. At the opposite end the church people gathered, looking rather uncomfortable and slightly embarrassed. Between the two groups there was literally a great gulf fixed! The microphone stood exactly in the middle of the lot, and we bravely began our meeting. We weren't getting anywhere, so we quickly abandoned the microphone and the pro-gramme, approached the boys, and began to ask them questions about their motorbikes. Eventually we began to talk about Christ and found them as open and as ready to listen as young people anywhere. We just had to be willing to talk "to" them instead of "at" them. The church folk gathered around, and we had a tremen-dous time. One of the young people offered to buy us a cup of coffee on the way home, so off we went to a huge motorway café that stood nearby.

Suddenly one of the boys said to our girls' group, "Hey, we didn't give you a chance to sing to us. Why don't you have a go now?"

Before I could get out of my coffee cup to protest, the girls jumped up and began travelling around the café like wandering minstrels, pausing at different tables and singing their Christian songs. I hid behind a pillar of the building and hoped no one would notice that we were together! Soon the manager bore down on us, and to my surprise and relief he informed me that he loved it! Would the young people come every week and sing! They would, and they did. The café held a thousand people and was always full in the summer months, especially during holidays. One day we asked the manager if we might use the café for a folk festival. He willingly agreed, charged us nothing for use of the facilities, and even suggested we charge 50p for entrance and give it to the missionaries! Thus began a programme that regularly reached hundreds of people, some of them amazed travellers, and incidentally paid for three years' missionary training for one of the warehouse's greatest girls.

Why, I mused, is "dying" so much fun! The Bible says, "Unless a kernel of wheat falls to the ground and dies, it remains only a single seed. But if it dies, it produces many seeds" (John 12:24). I was learning that the way to up is down, the way to life is death.

12

Lovest Thou Me?

"How would you like to be a pastor's wife?" my husband asked me. "A church in America has invited me to be their pastor." We had had such invitations before, but had never really seriously considered them. I had felt that Stuart's ministry belonged to the world. Why limit himself to one church and leave the wonderful worldwide opportunities he was being given?

For the next few weeks we received correspondence and phone calls from the leaders of this church, reaffirming their conviction that they believe it God's will that we should come.

"We're going to have to pray about it!" said Stuart cheerfully as he set off for another three-month preaching tour.

But how to pray? I found it difficult to pray from a neutral position! By now Stuart and I were separated for nine months of the year, and I had needed all my prayers to give me the power to stop crawling off the altar! With the possibility of more time together on the horizon, it became difficult to pray "Thy will be done" and mean it. Everything inside of me wanted so desperately for us to be together as a family.

Jesus had prostrated himself before his Father in Gethsemane and prayed thus, "If it be possible, let this cup pass from me." Having been honest before his Father, he had then used the "rope" of prayer to pull himself alongside the will of God, saying, "Nevertheless not my will but thine be done." I had to do the same. Looking ahead at the prospect of being an evangelist's wife all my life, I was honest!

"Oh, Father," I prayed, "let this cup pass from me, but nevertheless" – it took an awful long time getting said, but there it was – "not my will but thine be done. Please, Lord, give me the answer soon," I pleaded. "I don't think I can stay willing for either way very long!"

There were more reasons for wanting to go than the important personal need of a normal marital situation. For quite a while I had felt a sense of "completion" where the youth work was concerned. It was as if my job was finished, and I had worked myself out of a job. My co-worker had confided in me that she was strangely burdened and called to involve herself full-time in this ministry. She could easily assume the leadership if there were someone to take her place at mission headquarters. And it just "happened" that there was!

The children were the biggest factor of all. I felt I had failed in so many ways to be both father and mother to them – especially to our oldest boy, David, who was by now twelve years old. It was obvious he needed a man around. Our little girl, Judy, was also beginning to display signs of insecurity. I turned to the Word, fully expecting to read something like Luke 18:28–29:

> Peter said to him, "We have left all we had to follow you!"
>
> "I tell you the truth," Jesus said to them, "no one who has left home or wife or brothers or parents or children for the sake of the kingdom of God will fail to receive many times as much in this age and, in the age to come, eternal life."

I asked my Shepherd to lead us in right paths where his little lambs were concerned and sought special instructions.

Sitting on a beautiful English hillside beside a rushing, bubbling stream, I perused the Gospel of John. Approaching the end of the book, I still didn't feel I had received any directive.

I pleaded, "Lord, help me to go on reading until I sense your direction. You promised to show me the right path. Is it the right thing to do to put the children first this time? Please tell me." Continuing to read in John 21, I came to the question asked by the Lord, "Do you love me?" That was worth thinking about. Yes, I did love him, even though my love was weak and poor. As Peter answered, so did I, "Lord, You know my heart. I am fond of you!" Then he asked me as he had asked Peter long ago, "Do you truly love me more than these?" More than what? Than Stuart, than my homeland, my children and my people? More than these? I replied, "You know all things, Lord; I love you a little, and I want to love you more. I would like to think I love you first." I think the Shepherd smiled. Anyway, he gave me my answer: "Keep your love for me the most important thing in your life. 'Seek first his kingdom and his righteousness, and all these things will be given to you as well!' (Matthew 6:33). And now you will be shown the right path in this instance."

"Feed my lambs." There was my answer! It was repeated twice for emphasis. "My lambs," he had said. I knew who he was talking about: David, Judith and Peter. He was telling me they were his concern, and he had the very best in mind for them. He had planned for them in love. Seeing the birth of resentment in their hearts before I had ever noticed it, he had moved to make it possible for us to have the period of their growing teenage years together!

Running down the hillside back to our home, I was utterly convinced. After writing to my beloved mother to tell her of the possibility of our leaving, I next put a call through to Stuart in New York to tell him what the Lord had been revealing. My husband had left home feeling unconvinced about the wisdom of a move. But as he sat in New York in a big convention meeting the very night I called him, the preacher used a verse that convinced him of God's guidance about our decision. It was the same verse God had given me years before: "One [of you will] chase a thousand, and two put ten thousand to flight" (Deuteronomy 32:30, KJV). We were going to work together, and what was more we were going to "live" together – how exciting and challenging! We wired the church, accepting the call. Now all I had to do was pack up and be ready to move.

"All" I had to do! I began selling everything. We were to come to America with only our clothes. Everything else would be provided by the church, as this was by far the most practical way to move a family 3,000 miles. After all, I thought, this would be a good opportunity for me to practise what I had been preaching. I had often been quick to tell others that their treasure must be in heaven, and we must never set our hearts on "things", however lovely.

The snake sat on a packing case watching me. "All those nice china wedding presents," he mused. "I bet whoever gets them breaks them within a week!" All our beautiful antiques sold for practically nothing! We had been two short years in a cedar house that we had built with our own hands. My mother had generously furnished the home for us. It was beautiful and it was ours, but now it had to go. I was sure I wouldn't get a mansion nearly so nice in heaven! The snake added to my despondency by telling me that he thought he had seen one with my name on it up there that looked like a potting shed! I suddenly discovered that inanimate objects can come to mean far more than you realise. In a funny sort of way I was glad I had to prove I loved him more than "these".

The next testing time came when our visa was delayed. Waiting, I found out, was one of the hardest things for me to do. Was it divine delay or the snake? It was hard to tell. Then I fell ill and had to spend time in the hospital. They gave me a scrupulous going over, testing everything I possessed (and everything I didn't know I possessed), until they found the trouble and sent me home rejoicing. If we had gone to the U.S. any earlier, I would have landed in the hospital on arrival. Divine delay it surely had been. Almost immediately the visa was granted, and we went to London to get it. As we paused before a statue of Abraham Lincoln outside the imposing American embassy, we began to quiz our children.

"Now then, the ambassador may ask you who is the president of the United States," Stuart began.

"Oh, that's easy," replied one of the children. "Dick Van Dyke, of course!"

Seeing George Washington smiling down at their ignorance, I asked, "What's *he* famous for?"

After a long pause one of them stated hesitantly that he had invented the telephone! Despite this rather disturbing display of ignorance concerning the land to which we were about to embark, we were received cordially, asked no embarrassing questions whatsoever, and travelled triumphantly home as the proud possessors of our immigrant visas.

The goodbyes with our loved ones were hard, but the Lord provided a wonderful diversion at the last minute. Our beautiful golden retriever, Prince, was to accompany us to the U.S. Arriving late at the airport, we discovered the box we had ordered for him was far too small. We had "doped" Prince, and an argument ensued over the slightly dizzy dog, while the children and I boarded the plane. Relatives and friends watched in fascination as Stuart and the officials argued out on the runway. The people on the plane fumed at the delay!

"It's all because of our dog!" my daughter announced proudly, while I disappeared under the aeroplane seat with embarrassment!

Soon a larger box was obtained from somewhere, and Stuart entered the plane and took a seat. Nothing happened. Another official approached my husband,

and he left the plane again. Apparently the box was too large to fit into the hold. More delay. Then the door was shut, and off we went minus daddy and dog! Looking down at our waving relatives, we did not see Stuart. Then we learned that the kind pilot had invited Stuart and Prince into the cockpit!

When we arrived at London airport, a very drowsy dog preceded my husband down the cockpit steps, whereupon an elderly man behind me hissed, "Look at that poor man. He's blind!" Another commented, "There now, that's the way to deal with them hijackers!" We giggled our way into the airport, eventually found a new box, and praised the Lord for the amazing way he had provided the amusing distraction for us.

We were on our way. We faced the challenge of a new life in a new country. What would it be like? How would the children adjust? Would I be a good pastor's wife? I knew the Lord had led us this far and that he would be there to welcome us to our sphere of service. I had seen that he was El Shaddai – the God who was enough – and I knew from ten years' experience that none of us needed more than an "enough" God. Knowing that he would be there with all his adequacy for the immense challenge ahead, I wondered if there would be a snake in our parsonage?

13

Home Is the Will of God

"Thank goodness, there won't be much culture shock," I somewhat naively commented to my husband. "We don't even need to learn the language."

"You don't?" inquired the snake with a snicker.

So, there was a snake in the parsonage. I might have known! I noticed he had acquired an American accent that would enable him to slink more unobtrusively around our new environment. In his nasty way, he was spying out the land hoping to cash in on my arrival adjustments.

No culture shock?! The very first week I realised how wrong I had been. Answering the phone, I listened to a friendly voice inviting me to a "shower". Completely baffled and a little embarrassed (the only "shower" I was accustomed to was in the bathtub), I hesitated. Mistaking my silence for shyness, the kind lady hastily added, "There will be about 20 of us there altogether!" This only confirmed my suspicions. I'd heard about strange goings on among American women!

More confusion lay ahead. "Where are the dustbins?" I asked a surprised rubbish collector. "Please put my groceries in the boot of the car," I instructed a "bag boy". And later that day, seeking to quiet a noisy group of pre-teens who needed, in the American idiom, "to get it all together," I certainly achieved the desired results as I sharply told them to "pull their socks up".

Wandering through brightly lit, huge supermarkets among unrecognisable boxes searching for jam brands I'd never seen (jelly, I mean), I learned that our jelly was Jell-O, corn flour was cornstarch, biscuits were cookies, and English muffins were a food I'd never seen in England. I began to feel as though I'd just got married and was learning the rudiments of homemaking all over again.

It was fun, though, until everyone started telling us how they loved our accents. Didn't they realise *they* had the accents? *Our* speech was English! Then, to add insult to injury, I was introduced at a banquet (only in fun, of course) as a speaker with a speech impediment! What a good experience it was for us to be foreigners in a strange land and see and hear ourselves as others saw and heard us.

The children adjusted rapidly. *Very!* Peter, our youngest, arrived home from school after his first week of American education, announcing triumphantly, "Oh, mum, it's great! We don't have to say 'please' or 'thank you' any more!"

Judy had another problem. "*Who* are the nasty English redcoats?" she asked her father one day.

"Well, Judy," he replied, lifting her onto his knee, "there are two sides to every story, and this is the *wrong side!*"

Even the national holidays were different and often embarrassing. "Mr Briscoe," inquired a lady, "do you have a 4th of July in England?"

"No, Madam," he replied. "We go straight from the 3rd to the 5th!"

But it was not hard to feel welcomed and relaxed. Everyone seemed so friendly and interested in us.

"Nosy, you mean," hissed the snake.

"No, friendly!" I insisted.

I encountered love and encouragement, warmth and hospitality, and beautiful generosity on every hand. One token of this was a lovely home, painted and decorated, furnished and equipped, all ready to settle into and enjoy. The modern appliances stood like silent servants ready to obey. Matching bathroom towels and soap made bathing a joy. Surely we could settle down quickly and get on with the work God had transported us 3,000 miles to accomplish.

Why was it, I dared to ask myself, that an irritating sensation permeated my mind? I sought to analyse it and decided I just didn't feel permanent. In fact, with all the reasons in the world to be content and at rest, I just didn't feel settled at all. What was home, I asked myself. Was home family? Surely home *was* family, and for the first time we had the privilege of being together. How grateful we were for this new experience! Home was a measure of security and comfort perhaps, and we certainly had this in abundance. Home was a house, and so I certainly should have been 100 per cent at home in this beautiful abode. I felt guilty that my restlessness had to do with my not feeling at home in the house that had been provided, and I certainly suffered remorse for my unthankful attitude. Yet I was grateful. What was the answer to my problem?

Praying about my inner restlessness, I remembered Paul had prayed for the Ephesian Christians that Christ would settle down and feel at home in their lives. Was it possible that the Lord Jesus Christ could ever feel as I felt within "my" heart. I thought of him moving – much further than the mere 3,000 miles we had travelled. He had come from heaven's heights to the humble temple of my life. Here was the secret, and God began to show me the answer.

The inner rest and peace of heart could never be found in any earthly mansion, however beautiful. A heart-"settling" experience of rest and security would be mine only as I concentrated on settling him down in my life. It was not to be achieved through service for him, through speaking or teaching, or even through enjoying our new ministry and family life together. Did the holy Son of God feel at home in my heart? How could I know? What did I have to do to satisfy my heavenly guest?

One week later I discovered the answer. We had come to the U.S. with ten suitcases. Everything else we possessed had been sold or given away. One crate of precious items had been sent by sea and took six weeks to arrive. The crate contained a rather special English rug, a copper kettle, the children's teddy bears or special toys, and, of course, an English teapot and a package of prized English tea!

When the postman arrived with that crate, he must have thought we were crazy. Our excitement was ridiculous. We tore the big box apart, and each member of the family carried his beloved items into their prepared places. I heated the water, brewed my tea, and sat on our rug feasting my eyes on the little copper kettle. It was then that I recognised a deep inner conviction in my heart. I felt at *home* at last!

Why? Well, these things were *mine*. They had come from home, and *that's* what made all the difference. Suddenly I didn't feel as though I was on a permanent holiday anymore. This was it! I had arrived to stay.

My Lord spoke quietly to my happy heart. "It's the same with me. I entered your world without one suitcase. No ministering spirit accompanied me into the darkness of Mary's womb. I grew up in Nazareth without a familiar heavenly thing around me. All was strange to my divinity. Then I died and rose again to indwell the lives of all who would invite me. You know that however beautiful, well-painted and decorated those human dwelling places are, I never feel settled in them until my heavenly furniture arrives. A chair of love, a table of joy, and all the 'good works' a wholly regenerated person should be thoroughly furnished with. As a man, as a woman, as a child settles *me* down, I will settle *them* down because home is the will of God, and the will of God is to make me at home."

So, I took time to be still and concentrate on my relationship with Jesus. I sought to make sure he was comfortable in his home and asked him to get the heavenly moving van going to furnish my life with his familiar things.

I felt pretty guilty about this little inner struggle and wondered if anyone had sensed my problem and interpreted my behaviour as unthankfulness for this labour of love in providing our home. I was conscious of the importance of keeping our home as beautiful as possible. So many, many people made their way through the house, and all had an understandable curiosity to peek in each room. After all, so many had had a part in the time-consuming preparation. It was the *church's* home, not *ours*!

"Nosy interference," hissed the snake.

"No, understandable curiosity," I replied firmly.

Owing to a lack of church facilities, the senior Sunday school met in our house at 9.30 am each week and occupied most of the rooms. Then we attended church service, after which I often served as many as fifteen for Sunday lunch. One Sunday evening we were to entertain some of our church leaders. So I marshalled the children and commanded them to assist me in clearing up the battlefield. "Just grab all the debris and stuff it into the big cupboard in the kitchen," I instructed them. This being their sort of cleaning, they happily complied just in time for me to appear poised and serene to welcome our guests. I invited them to view the house while I brewed the tea.

One dear lady assisted me in the kitchen. Just then the telephone rang, and I went to answer it. I watched aghast as we began opening drawer after drawer, cupboard after cupboard trying to find a kitchen implement. Clutching the phone and feeling quite ill, I actually watched the snake pulling her hand toward the over-stuffed corner cupboard!

She opened it and was deluged with a shower of miscellaneous objects: wet trainers, the dog's dishes, and the like. I turned red, white and blue, which, while being patriotic, didn't help! The snake was nearly sick with mirth – laughter being a rare phenomenon to him. I noticed he stopped abruptly as he watched me preparing to be truly honest.

"Well," I said, carefully replacing the phone, "now you know what sort of a housewife I am!" Bless their hearts! Those ladies laughed and loved me just the same – even though my corner cupboard was full of junk! I needn't have pretended to play the part. I had taken the first difficult step in learning an important lesson. I learned that as I was living in a goldfish bowl, I wasn't to try being anything but the fish that I was! How foolish to pretend to be a cat or a dog! I had to learn to be myself and allow them to see I was human.

"Check around," the snake advised everyone. "If she wants to show you how human she is, I'll do all I can to help!" I didn't doubt that for one minute! After they had all gone home, the snake suggested to me that I'd really have to try a little harder. Being satisfied with showing my "humanness" wasn't good enough. "You'll have to impress them – live up to their expectations of you. Put on an act just a 'little bit'," he wheedled.

The Lord Jesus contradicted him, laughed at my red face, and reminded me that hypocrite and actor come from the same root word. "My church is full of hyp-ocrites," he commented. "Don't add to it! Pretending you are something other than what you are only makes a liar out of you," he pointed out. "Don't try and keep a corner cupboard in your life filled with junk. Give me the run of your house, full permission to help you tidy up the mess, and don't try to stuff it away and hide it from *me*! I'm here to help you pick up the house, not to pretend the mess doesn't exist. You must be prepared to be as open and honest with your people as you are with me; then they'll empathise. Then you can grow together without constantly living a lie."

How often we set ourselves up to be paragons of virtue. "I've given *all*," our lips say, while the corner cupboard, a silent testimony, stands full of hidden junk! "Oh, Lord, open it," I prayed.

14

Burying the Pastor's Wife

I noticed that at social gatherings I was introduced as "the pastor's wife". Each time it happened the snake snickered and pointed out that the other women present were not introduced as "the grocer's wife" or "the road sweeper's wife" or "the rubbish collector's wife"! "You're stuck with it," he hissed happily. "Every time you're given your title, a preconceived notion flashes across their minds. All of them will have varied ideas of just how you ought to 'perform', and as each will differ according to their church and cultural backgrounds, you will have to be a freak to keep them all happy!"

I thought about that. It was true. I, myself, had had my own preconceived notions of a lady with such a title. I had imagined a shadowy, mouselike "personage living in the parsonage," skulking about in the wings of a dilapidated creaky house – hair firmly screwed into a bun, her flat shoes facilitating the many errands of mercy she must run. These "errands" were as vague in my mind as the personage herself! What was she so tirelessly and piously busy doing? Succouring the dying, mending other people's cast-off clothes for the poor missionaries (only the best for God's front-line workers!), pressing the parson's Sunday suits all day Saturday, and helping with the annual sale of work to pay for a new church steeple to house more mice and bats?

"Help!" I gulped. "Please, Lord, not that!"

The snake was really enjoying himself by now. He'd been working in his underground darkroom and had produced not only a set of pictures of the pastor's wife at "home", but also a set of pictures of the pastor's wife at "work". These he proceeded to share with me.

"You must please the church," he intoned. "This is your first duty." Of course, the snake doesn't care who you please as long as you don't bring pleasure to the heart of God. The church is an excellent substitute, especially if you are "religious" and wouldn't be tempted to please "the world". "They have a right to expect certain things of you," he continued. "First of all, you *must* play the piano!" At this he nearly swallowed his horrid forked tongue in mirth!

"Well, that's *one* way I'd be certain *not* to please the church," I commented, "unless they want all their hymns played with one finger!"

Quite carried away, the snake continued. "A pastor's wife must sit in the leadership chair at every women's gathering. She must teach in the Sunday school (whether or not she has an impediment in her speech) and must never correct her children in public!"

I'd had enough. I decided the first funeral to be conducted by me, not my husband, would be a ceremony when I would once and for all bury the image of "the pastor's wife" under the life-giving soil of the Word of God.

What did God's Word say about the matter? I turned to 1 Corinthians 12 and found that the apostle Paul didn't want us to be ignorant about our spiritual gifts. I knew that the pastor's wife had the same responsibility toward God as every other church member – to discover her spiritual gift and to exercise it. But I also knew there were certain duties that went along with her privileged position for which she might not be gifted.

I didn't feel altogether ignorant as to my gifts. From past experience I knew that I had been blessed in starting things, exploding situations, moving into new areas in evangelistic outreach. I knew I had a gift of teaching and speaking and a gift of creative ideas for children and teens. But I was not a gifted administrator or committee member; I was not a good listener; and I could produce little "small talk" in company. Seeing that the latter gifts seemed to be the most obvious ones that would be required for my pastoral duties, I had considerable trepidation in my heart.

"Maybe these gifts would develop as I exercised them," I mused. Maybe I did possess them and just didn't know it. I thought back to the days at Capernwray Hall and the maxim God had taught me then. "The best way to begin is to begin." So I decided to begin and see!

But *where* should I begin? Should I just wait till someone asked me to do something? How did I get going? There were two extremely gifted ladies teaching the women's studies at church, so maybe the area of teenage activities would be a good place to start. There was no set meeting for them anyway. I began to work with a team of teens using our English musical drama *Sitting on the Fence*. Many adults helped me, and for the first time I enjoyed having adequate mature leadership.

But I did notice that Europeans and Americans had different ideas about leadership. It appeared to be a lot more "democratic" here than at home. I had been used to a leader leading and others following. The leader then constantly worked herself out of a job – not (I hasten to add) so she could recline on a spiritual bed of ease, but so she could lead off in another unexplored direction! I came to realise that I was leaving a lot of confused and hurt people in my wake, and after some painful situations I had to reassess my "scriptural" ideas of spiritual leadership. I began a personal study on the subject.

I discovered many things, the most important being that love is the answer. A leader *loves*. "Do you love only what you like?" inquired my heavenly leader. "Or do you love the unlovely?"

"I love only what I like," I answered honestly.

"Well, now," said the Lord, "you do have me living within you, and I'm an expert at loving the unlovely or I wouldn't have stayed so long in the temple of your heart! The love of God is shed abroad by the Holy Spirit which is given to you. He will touch your hard, unloving heart and recreate a warm, loving one inside instead."

"How?" I inquired.

He answered with one word: "Alone."

"Alone?" I questioned. "What do you mean?"

I turned over the pages of my Bible exposing my mind, spirit and soul to the Word. I read about the mourning Master depicted in the account in Matthew 14 when he learned of John the Baptist's death.

John and Jesus had run, had played, had romped through childhood together in Nazareth. John and Jesus had talked, had dreamed, had wept, had planned their days of ministry upon this needy planet.

John had gladly sent his dearest disciples to follow Jesus instead of ministering to him, and there upon the bank of his baptistry he had announced his Lord's presence. "Behold *him*, not me. I'm not worthy to lick his boots! My cousin, yes, but more than human cousin – heaven's Lamb who takes away the sin of the world."

"Baptise me, John!" commanded Christ.

"But I have need to be baptised of *Thee!*" John confessed. "Like all poor fallen humans (even though none greater than the Baptist had ever walked the earth according to Christ's testimony), I have need," he said. And so, cast into prison, kept by foul Herod, chained and beaten, the brave man continued to thrill the heart of God.

"Herod! You shall not have your brother Philip's wife," he thundered. And brother Philip's wife had had enough and planned a dinner party with the head of the prophet John as an entree! Then came his disciples who took up the body, buried it, and went and told Jesus (which is always the best thing for us to do whenever we take up a dear human body and bury it). When Jesus heard of it, he departed into a desert place *alone* to weep for John's last torture, Elizabeth and Zacharias, and death!

How Jesus needed time alone! "My greatest transactions took place alone," my Lord told me. "Tell me, Jill, what's taken place lately alone with you?" There was a heavy silence. I had no answer. Not much, I thought! "It's alone I can touch you with the 'feelings' of other people's infirmities," my Lord continued. That really struck home to me. I'd always thought that verse in Hebrews said, "He was touched with people's infirmities," but it doesn't. It says, "He was touched with the 'feelings' of people's infirmities."

So often I had sung with emotion the words of the lovely song: "He touched me, oh, he touched me." But had he touched me? That *only* happens alone. Alone, grief is not allowed to sour into self-pity. Alone, he'll touch us and make us sad; touch us and make us cry; touch us with righteous indignation against wrong doing; touch us with the "feelings" of others' troubles.

"Are there people you are trying to lead, Jill? Are there people you are trying to touch through the people you are trying to lead? Are there people near and dear to you in your own family circle whom you long to have touched? Well, they won't be touched until you are touched! If I can only have permission to get to you, then I'll get to them!"

"But, Lord," I complained, "I've got enough infirm feelings of my own without collecting other people's." It was then God challenged me with the multitude.

"Jill, the need of the multitude is as great today as it was in this incident. Men, women, boys, girls – a multitude of need. They must be fed, taught, cared for and, above all, loved. When I was interrupted by the multitude that day, I had been truly *alone*. The result was that

I was moved with compassion. And that word 'moved' means convulsed! Are you convulsed with compassion for the multitude? If you're not, ask yourself what has been happening alone."

I thought of my busy day. It had started with a hectic morning, settling into a new country and a new house. The phone rang continually: long-distance calls, short-distance calls, calls of distress and calls of mundane detail. Our youngest arrived in the middle of my preparation to tell me a wild joke, while the older two scrapped on the rug over something or nothing. The dog had escaped early in the day, and now Peter came to tell me our retriever had returned bringing with him four people's doormats. I had a vision of stealthily restoring them at dusk. At this point our water pipes burst. I looked at Peter and contemplated the multitude of interruptions, and I was surely moved, but certainly *not* with compassion.

"Peter!" I shook him. "My little multitude!" Looking at me somewhat surprised, he retreated to Judy's room saying, "Hey, mummy just called me a little multitude!"

I knew my aloneness had been fake. Nothing had happened between my Lord and me or I, too, could have faced my multitude of need with true understanding and compassion.

I thought about the miracle of multiplication in the Bible story of the feeding of the five thousand. The "untouched" disciples had been commanded to feed the needs of the people. Having had a quick committee meeting and looked at the budget, they knew they were totally inadequate and had nothing whatsoever to give. Sure, they cared, but not enough. They didn't care like he cared.

"Give them something to eat," he commanded.

"Send them away. Let them get it from someone else," they replied. "We're bankrupt!"

The Bread of Life sadly stood by, grieved because they reckoned completely without him. Their excuses were sensible, practical, thoughtful and obvious.

"We're not bakers. We're fishermen. It's just not our gift to manufacture bread!"

"But I'm not asking you to make it," said Jesus. "Just to market it. I'll make it. You take it from me and pass it around. Get near enough to me so I can take you in my hands like those loaves and fishes. Let me touch you, and when I do I'll bless you and break you and give you to the people. Then they will all be satisfied. They will know you love them. You touch me; I'll touch you; you'll touch them." Leaders who will love must know what it is to be *alone*.

I thought of that little boy standing tall and straight, looking lovingly into the face of Jesus. "You're free to help yourself," he said. And he meant it! Not just my fish and loaves – my pitiful inadequacy in the face of multitudes of need – my heart, my feelings, my life, my all.

Jesus, I noticed, *took* it all! That's the only way to get the multitude fed.

"Can't I just keep *one* little loaf? That favourite one just for me?" I asked. "Can't I serve you without loving like you?" Before I asked, I knew the answer. I must let him take all and touch me. He did. It hurt, but then it was that the miracle of multiplication began.

"Remember: The pastor's wife is a person (though she be married to the parson)," the Lord concluded.

"Find your gift and exercise it. Study the Word for the principles and 'come apart' *alone* so that I may touch you and you may love."

"Please the church," screeched the snake.

"Please me," commanded Jesus. "And then, give them something to eat!"

15

They're Leaving the Church

A dear pastor friend of ours had taken Stuart and me aside after learning we were about to take a pastorate and wisely told us, "In your new position, there will be a honeymoon period. When the honeymoon is over, watch for a crisis to arise over even the most trivial of issues. People will then leave the church. Don't panic. And – if you can possibly avoid it – *never* get into either a building programme or a change in the church constitution!"

With his words ringing in our ears, we waited for the honeymoon to be over. The only problem was finding out just when it was finished because it never seemed to start! After being in the church just a few short weeks, an important church officer resigned.

"He needs a vote of confidence, that's all," the church leaders informed us. I felt it was we who needed the vote of confidence!

"I'm afraid I don't feel confident about a man who resigns almost as soon as the new pastor arrives," my husband responded.

"Accept his resignation!" The honeymoon sighed and tiptoed out of sight! The following day we heard, "They're leaving the church." We came to realise this little phrase was the title of one of the snake's "top 10" records. He plays it in countless pastors' ears. The words of the song come to the pastor's family in whispered tones, passed on from one voice to another or in unison as a congregation.

Immediately you have a vision of a packed pew with a yawning gap in the centre which draws the immediate attention of everyone in the service. The pastor is then put in the position of not knowing what to do. Is the rumour true? Does he or she get a chance to talk the issue over, or is the pastor suddenly confronted with empty spaces before fully realising what is happening? And if he or she is well informed from a reliable and unbiased source, does the pastor then heroically cast himself in front of the metaphorical church door saying "over my dead body"?

Well, we soon learned that to run after everyone who was rumoured to be "leaving the church" meant acquiring a spiritual Olympic running record. As the pastor's wife, I was definitely against running. It was much easier to face the empty spaces than the angry faces! Also, the snake had the most irritating habit of standing at my elbow as the offended person approached and putting the most snakelike ideas into my head, such as "When you shake hands, crush her fingers!" or "Kick her in the shins." It was hard for me to cope with the people who decided to stay and make their grievances known.

To my surprise, my husband coolly encouraged anyone who wished to leave to do so. "Both doors of our church are open. The front and the back!" became his motto. I decided to stand at the front door to shake hands in the future!

The snake had immediately noticed my overreaction to criticism of my husband. He knew it was a far harder thing for me to take than criticism of myself. He planned to use this to his advantage, and it wasn't long before he had an opportunity to do so.

Within a year of our arrival at the church we found ourselves in the middle of a major issue: a change in the church constitution! Sitting in a pretty highly charged, emotional church meeting, I realised how deeply people were feeling. There was much discussion over a doctrinal point that to me was a secondary issue, having nothing to do with salvation. I watched people literally "leaving the church" from that gathering, and I was completely floored by the whole thing. The snake saw his chance and took it.

"It's a shame," he hissed sympathetically. "Why don't they ask their spiritual leader's advice? Why won't they respect his great biblical knowledge? Get up on your feet and stand up for your husband. He needs you to help him out of this hole!"

Now, one thing my husband didn't need at that moment in time was intervention. But up I got, managed two sentences, then burst into tears!

"Poor thing," smirked the snake, handing me a copy of the church constitution with which to blow my nose. "Try again!"

I managed to ignore him and retreat to the ladies' room where I had some prayer with a Christian friend. When I returned red-eyed to the scene of my disaster, the church was in prayer. The crisis was over – the people had left – and I had begun to learn some new and necessary lessons.

First, after prayer and guidance we must do what we really believe the Lord is leading us to do. We only wanted the best for his work in this place. At the same time, we had to respect other people's views and feelings and in no way allow their departure from our fellowship to make any difference in our attitudes and relationships with them. That was the hard thing.

I remembered the rebellion of King David's son Absalom and his eventual downfall. I thought about the edict permitting him to dwell in the king's city for three long years yet never being allowed to see the king's face. Can you tell me King David knew no sorrow? Of course he did. So did a repentant Absalom. Deep anguish and confusion of heart accompany any schism in "the family".

I learned to *face* people after violent confrontation. This is an important thing to do. To be mature enough to agree to differ or to agree to disagree without being disagreeable is a miracle only the Spirit of grace can accomplish.

The test came the first time I encountered a person who had left our fellowship. It was in the supermarket. There she was buying bread, and I had an almost irresistible desire to bury myself in the green vegetables and try to look like a lettuce until she passed by! The Lord helped me approach her and happily inquire if her family had found a church home where their needs were being well met. I suddenly realised that she was more embarrassed than I and seemed genuinely pleased I'd made a move toward her. We chatted, and she told me they were well settled into a good church fellowship with which they could more happily identify, and I told her quite sincerely how glad I was it had all worked out well. We have remained good friends.

I learned that I *must* take the initiative if and when the opportunity occurred. But I also learned to pray and wait for the opportunities. Often I needed to grow in my attitude or knowledge of the situation. In our human families some members have to grow up some before harmony is achieved, and the Spirit often cautions us to wait if one party isn't quite ready for a fence-mending operation.

Humility was the key. The humility of each esteeming others better than themselves (Philippians 2:3). And also a practical determination to be cheerfully friendly whenever an encounter occurred "after" the event.

The main temptation I had to combat was to refrain from a telephone campaign. My reaction to criticism of my husband or myself was one of immediate self-justification, self-righteousness, and a determination tovindicate us in the eyes of a friend. No one likes stones thrown at them.

"But one can always pick them up and throw them back," the snake interposed. "Retaliation is scriptural," he continued. "Jesus took a whip and threw the money changers out of the temple, remember?" I thought about that. The snake, of course, was misquoting Scripture again, so I knew I needed to look at the context.

Jesus never retaliated on his own behalf, only on behalf of his heavenly Father or on behalf of the poor and oppressed. These people who were leaving our church were people the Lord Jesus had died for and loved as much as he loved me. Sometimes I found that hard to accept! If we are honest, we have to admit that we don't really believe God could love *anyone* as much as he loves us! But he does. What's more, even if others are doing something that grieves God, are we any better? Are we always right in thought, word and deed?

How easy to be like the self-righteous Pharisees who took the woman caught in adultery and placed her in the midst of their enlisted mob of sympathisers and picked up stones of condemnation to hurl at her! It happened in the temple – even in the presence of the Lord Jesus himself.

My Lord took me to John 8:1–11 and spoke to my heart concerning such verbal stone-throwing. "Put your stones down, Jill, unless you are without sin. Judge not lest you be judged."

"They're leaving the church." We would hear it many times. And each time we would have to search our hearts to seek God's mind and follow his leading. We must respect the other persons and their important points of view. We are responsible only for our attitudes, not for the attitudes of others. And we are *never*, no never, to pick up stones!

I caught her in the act!
*She **lied** to me.*
*I rushed her to my friends. They shouted **"Guilty!"***
I stooped down to the ground to pick up stones of
*   condemnation,*

Then saw the writing in the dust – my Saviour's
     proclamation:
Without sin? Throw!
With sin? Go!
Before I cast my stones at thee.
I've caught you in that act –
You've lied to **me***!*
And in the courts of heaven they shouted **"Guilty!"**

I caught him in the act.
Adultery.
I told the gaping crowd. They sneered and sniggered.
I stooped down to the ground to pick up stones of
     accusation.
But saw the writing in the dust – my Saviour's
     proclamation:
Have you been true?
Heart and mind through?
The thought is worthy of the act.
You stand unfaithful too,
To him and **Me***.*
And from the courts of heaven echoed **"Guilty!"**

He caught me in the act of all that's sinful
And ushered me to the spires of heaven.
The angels stooped to pick up stones of righteous
     indignation,
Then saw the blood drops in the dust that spelled
     justification*:*
Go – sin no more.
These stones you store
Within your heart leave here with me.
Judge not, lest ye be judged.
And in the courts of heaven they shouted **"Glory!"**

16

Retreat to Advance

We were settling in well, I thought. The children were happy. The work was expanding, and I hadn't made too many unforgivable blunders. I was enjoying working with the teens on our musical drama. It was a challenge, and teens were obviously my niche. Then it happened! A knock on the door, a charming lady, and a warm invitation to come to her home, meet her neighbours, and tell them about Christ.

There didn't seem to be any harm in that. One little meeting would be all right, even if the lady didn't belong to our church. She visited regularly, and if her friends wanted some questions answered, I would be happy to oblige.

Arriving at the lady's beautiful home, I discovered a room comfortably full of talented and intelligent ladies. I gave my testimony, got up to leave, and was asked to return to teach the Bible.

"What do you want me to teach you?" I inquired.

"Answer our questions."

"What questions?"

"Why does God allow suffering? Why do some people still believe in hell? Why is the Old Testament still read today when it's obviously out of date? How do you find God? What is a Christian?"

I couldn't believe they wouldn't know the scriptural answers to these things. But apparently they didn't, or they wouldn't be asking! Surely it wouldn't do any harm to take a few weeks and do a basic doctrine study with them. I suggested working through my husband's basic Bible study on Christian doctrine entitled "Discovering God". They were so sweet and enthusiastic, and the next class saw more ladies than ever. By the end of six weeks approximately 60 of them were meeting regularly.

The snake slithered happily home with me one day and hissed, "Now you're in for it. Don't you realise what you've done? There's not *one* lady from *your* church there. These ladies all belong to another church, and what's more, you are teaching them things their minister may not like. How dare you sneak in among his flock subverting his sheep! And then there are your own church ladies. Wait until they hear about all that you are doing. I'll make sure I put all the right ideas in their minds about your motives. I'll make them jealous and sow seeds of misunderstanding all over the place." He ran out of words. His horrid little eyes were glistening as he visualised the damage. I didn't doubt his ability for one moment!

As I thought about it all, one of our own women's Bible teachers resigned because of ill health, and I was asked to take over! My immediate reaction was to drop my class and do so. My husband, as usual cooler and calmer than I, sounded a note of caution. He knew it was taking me hours of study to keep ahead of my enthusiastic students, and there was no way I could do all the necessary Scriptural preparation and cope with the youth work as well, without neglecting my responsibilities at home. He suggested I continue the study but take it out of the homes into a neutral meeting place. This way we could consolidate. The church's women could come also, and the teaching work that had begun could continue with a better use of time. After all, we could hardly bring 60 ladies from other churches into Elmbrook!

"But what will 'they' say?" I asked.

"If it's of the Lord, he will put his seal upon it," Stuart said.

"But what a start to my relationship with our church women," I argued.

"You didn't seek this. You just took an opportunity. Now follow his leading," was his reply.

The snake was furious. I don't know how much of the future he knows, but he obviously knew enough to see the blessing ahead. He was at my side constantly, making sure he passed on all the discouraging comments he heard around church. I knew some of our ladies disapproved, and I so desperately wanted them to be part of it all.

We took the meeting into the basement of a bank, and the attendance grew to over 100 women. Next, we rented a theatre in a local shopping centre, and after two years we rejoiced to find 400 women coming week after week to study the Word of God. Our church ladies were great and eventually became the backbone of our interdenominational committee.

The snake hated the theatre. He much preferred a little meeting room somewhere with a lot of overfed Christians being stuffed yet stuffier! He hated the hunger and the interest and the renewal of so many lovely women. He hated the way some were born again, marriages were healed and prayers were answered. He hated it all. I didn't underestimate him. I knew he wouldn't just sulk in the back seat of the theatre. We are told not to be ignorant of his devices. We need to watch and pray!

Finishing our series of Bible studies in May, we decided to join together with two other Bible teachers from our church and have a one-day retreat. We had no idea what was in store. We managed to obtain the use of a lovely Roman Catholic college and gave our studies a name for the day – "The Liberated Woman". It received widespread press interest and even TV and radio coverage. We watched as 900 women signed up.

We stumble by surprise on so many of God's great purposes! He wanted the city won for him while we were far too partial in our outlook. What next? We decided we would have more Bible study and then a combined two days of retreat. That was a step of faith in itself to have a retreat in January in snowy Wisconsin! It kept the women on their knees, that was for sure. The two days were to be identical programmes. This time we rented a huge new exposition centre and managed to keep the price down to three dollars per person. The programme ran from 8.30 am to 3.00 pm, combining lectures, small group discussions, prayer, music and testimonies, fellowship and sharing. The Lord gave us 2,100 women over the two days.

"Where do we go from here, Lord?" we asked. The question in our minds was, "Do we just get bigger and bigger or should we grow by spreading the time over more days instead?" The programme appeared to need variation. "We'll try a weekend first and then a whole week of women's convention next year – how about that?" I suggested. The gallant committee answered, "Let's go," so we set off to plan and pray.

Meanwhile, wonderful doors of opportunity were opening up for me – speaking engagements that would take me all over the country. Up until now Stuart had been the traveller and I had stayed at home. Now it was to be a little different. The snake saw his opportunity and took it, of course.

17

Have Bible, Will Travel

The snake fastened his seat belt carefully and settled back for take-off. He pointed out how the windows rattled and the floor shook and how the right wing didn't look too safe to him at all. "Have you noticed how the wings vibrate?" he inquired of me earnestly. I turned pale. All that flapping about seemed a bit dangerous to me. Surely it would weaken the joints!

"Why don't you move into the aisle seat," he suggested next. "It might balance things up a bit. Haven't you noticed how everyone is sitting along one side?"

Now, this was getting quite ridiculous! Here I was a complete bag of nerves. I hated flying. My heart was thumping, and I felt quite sick with fright every time there was a bump. I tried to be logical and remember my husband's reassurance on a previous trip. "You won't go to heaven one moment before you're meant to!" I just thought the moment I was "meant to go" had arrived. I got out my Bible and notes and started reading to take my mind off the journey. The subject I had been asked to teach was – *faith*! One little five-letter word – *faith*! Trust? Dependence? How could I possibly speak on that when I was reduced to a shivering heap of jelly by an aeroplane trip?

"Lord," I prayed, "You're going to have to give me victory before I get off this plane or I will have nothing whatsoever to share with these ladies!" And he did. One little phrase from my husband's message that Sunday returned to me. He had made the statement: "The initial avenue of spiritual experience is the mind." Then the Lord brought one verse of Scripture to remembrance: "I will trust and not be afraid" (Isaiah 12:2). My mind told me the object of my faith was trustworthy. I got my intellectual feet on that rock – then I applied my will. "I will trust. I will not be afraid, starting from now," I announced loudly in the snake's ear. He hastily disappeared into the seat pocket. The emotions followed – *peace*. I can honestly testify that God dealt with my fear of flying that day. Praise him! It was also helpful to share that experience with the women during my talk on faith the first evening of the conference.

At my first big ladies' meeting, I had an unnerving experience. Feeling decidedly unsure of myself, I wandered into the reception area. No one recognised "the guest speaker", of course. So I stood there looking hopeless and helpless. All sorts of panicky feelings began to take over. The first session alleviated some of them, and I began to relax.

As soon as the counselling was over, a lady approached me and invited me to her room. She then announced that she wanted to cast the demon out of me! I looked at her and my mouth fell open! I felt quite hysterical for a moment and then was able to assure her that I didn't have a demon and asked her where she had been hearing about demons. She appeared to be extremely confused. The way the Lord gave me Scriptures to counsel her was a real encouragement to my own soul. Over and over again at these conferences I was to meet all sorts of women with many "extreme" theological ideas. I became more and more convinced that a balanced knowledge of the Word was the answer.

I studied my Bible as I'd never studied before. I had to know the answers to the questions before the questions ever came. I must be balanced myself. I needed to learn the whole counsel of God. I realised an overemphasis on any doctrine of Scripture is a potential breeding ground for heresy, and I had to do my homework.

I began to enjoy the weekend conferences. I was determined to push away the snake's photo displays of confusion at home: the vision of Judy falling off her bike, or David and Peter having fights no one refereed, or Stuart not being able to find either of his preaching suits because I'd forgotten to pick them up from the cleaners! Once I'd been away a few times and had not been met by weeping deprived children, I realised things were fine.

Relaxed, I could now benefit from the fine teaching of my fellow speakers. Enriched and challenged by new ideas and methods of evangelism, I could return home to share these relevant ideas with our own ladies. I felt so privileged to get to know many of God's special people. However, I was often overcome with a sense of the ridiculous. Usually it happened just before I had to get up to speak.

The snake would whisper in my ear, "Who are *you*, anyway? What Bible training have you had? What are your qualifications for speaking with such great authority from the depths of your ignorance?" Then the Lord's quiet assurance would come: "Her qualifications are my commission to go and make disciples and her enabling is the Holy Spirit. Who shall lay anything to the charge of God's elect? It is God that justifies. Who is he that condemns?" It was then I remembered that one of the snake's names is the "accuser of the brethren". The snake wasn't the only accuser of the brethren, or rather the sisters! Others took a similar line.

"I suffer not a woman to speak!" How can you expect God to bless you when you flagrantly disobey his Word?"

The snake was quick to follow up the advantage. "Don't you remember the time you were speaking to the students at Capernwray Hall about youth work and those four upstanding new converts, all men, left the lecture hall because a woman was teaching? They knew you shouldn't be doing it!"

I remembered all right. That had hurt! How did they think I could speak with such peace and joy in my heart if I was sinning?

I knew different denominations held different views about female speakers. They varied considerably. I, myself, disliked listening to most women speakers. I'd rather listen to a man on most occasions. But what *did* the Word say? It appeared to be a relevant subject that needed looking into, since I was receiving numerous invitations not only to address teens and women, but "mixed" groups as well.

This was not a new problem to me. Almost as soon as I became a Christian I heard opposing views about the matter. One group I met with refused to let women even pray aloud in a mixed group, and yet this same church allowed their missionary women to preach, teach and pray far away on the mission field. That didn't appear to be very consistent, and it also gave me the feeling that God liked using men instead of women who were obviously second-rate material! I knew this was not scriptural, as the Bible plainly states in Christ there is neither male nor female – all are one in Christ Jesus. Then again, women were forbidden to speak to a group of men but were expected to witness on a one-to-one basis! What difference did the plurality make, I wondered.

Paul obviously listened to Philip's daughters, all four of whom were busy exercising their speaking gifts. There was no rebuke recorded in the Scriptures from Paul on the occasion of his visit with them. The context of the relevant verses in the Scriptures had to be considered, too, against the culture of the times.

The big scriptural prohibition appeared to be the principle of usurping the authority of the man. If, therefore, the men of a fellowship in whom the care and oversight of the flock had been entrusted invited me to exercise my spiritual gift among them, I could know I would not be usurping their authority. If, on the other hand, I marched into an assembly uninvited and stood to preach, I would certainly be out of order.

I believe whenever men of God recognise the gifts of God in women of God and encourage them, under their leadership and guidance, to exercise these gifts, the work of God is expanded.

I was not prepared for the next attack of the snake. It was pretty subtle. I was to share the podium at a large meeting with another speaker I had never met or worked with before. The moment I was introduced to her I found myself instantly reacting, and I was not honest enough to call my reaction what it was.

The snake, who has rare flashes of honesty (only, of course, when it suits his purposes), faced me with the truth: "You don't like her. You don't even want to sit and listen to her speak. And how can you possibly take the meeting tomorrow with that attitude?"

While this woman was speaking, I began to read the Word asking the Lord for a direct rebuke. I got one! Coming to Matthew 12:48, 50 I read Jesus' words: "Who is my mother, and who are my brothers? ... For whoever does the will of my Father in heaven is my brother and sister and mother." Well now, this dear lady was *family*. She was my sister! She was busy doing the will of God. As in earthly families, I realised I would be closer to some sisters than others, but the bond was there. I asked the Lord for the right sisterly feelings and immediately received a warm appreciation for the woman. Thereafter we had a great time together. God's forever family is forever, so I guess the closer we get acquainted down here the more we shall enjoy each other up there!

Another temptation I found I needed to combat regarded the subject matter I was to present. So many of my co-speakers had such wonderfully dramatic testimonies.

"Maybe you could colour yours up a bit," the snake helpfully suggested. "After all, you are 3,000 miles away from home and nobody will know!"

Exaggeration has always been a problem with me. Too often I indulgently call it my wild imagination instead of lies! The snake continued taunting me with the fact that dry Bible stuff wouldn't hold their attention after listening to someone relating how she had murdered her mother with an axe! I would find myself looking over my notes again and again. Maybe I should tell more stories. Maybe I could dramatise it more. Was the straight exposition of the Word of God sufficient to hold people's interest? Back from its precious pages I received my answer: "My Word shall not return to me empty. My Word is a light and a lamp for people who are frightened of their personal darkness. My Word is like a fire burning up the dross of people's lives and like a hammer demolishing the rock resistance of hardened attitudes. My Word is a seed growing in the rubbish dumps of wasted territory, producing flowers and fragrances instead of weeds and thorns."

I was to preach the Word, not my experience! Here and there illustrations from my experience would help to explain the Word, but I learned my lesson well. He promised to bless the promises of his Word, not the preaching of my experiences!

Time and time again I watched the power of the Word produce not emotion, but conviction. There was a difference.

Near my home in England there was a little graveyard. In the ancient plot lay an extraordinary grave.
The old stone had been split asunder, and through the
middle of it rose a huge oak tree, its branches lifted
toward the sun. Sometime in the past, one little acorn
buried in the earth beneath that stone, possessing the
fantastic dynamic of life, had found the incredible
power to split the stone wide open. It was the Word
that had accomplished that very same thing in my life.
The dynamic of life in the seed of the Word of God. It
had been the truths of the Bible that had brought life
from death in my own personal graveyard.

Almost at once the Lord taught me to pray for "conviction" of sin that would last, not emotion that would
soon be past. Conviction is the Holy Spirit's business.
He will convict the world of sin, of righteousness and
judgement. The Bible teaches that this conviction usually manifests itself as an emotional low, not an emotional high, and is absolutely necessary before God's
promises can bring release and peace of mind. What
could I give these ladies that would hold them fast a
few weeks away from the experience of a retreat?
Doctrine, teaching, facts: the *Word*. In temptation, they
would need the *Word*. In witness, they would need the
statement of the *Word*. This I would give and refuse the
temptation to paint an untrue picture of a wildly
depraved life with all the accompanying gory details.

A new motto was born: Have Bible – will travel.
Have Word – will tell. Have peace – will triumph! "Go
ye and make disciples," he said. And so I did!

18

The Wine Tasting

Elijah had had a good morning in church. The whole of Israel had turned out for the service, and it was a pretty fiery sermon. Literally! God had demonstrated his power in a supernatural way, and Elijah had finished off the prophets of Baal in a gory after-meeting. Facing Ahab, weak "King Compromise", Elijah told him to get back to his chariot and head home because the rains were coming.

Now the sky had never been bluer, the sun never hotter, the sand never dustier, but Elijah possessed the ears of faith. He heard the sound of abundance of rain. Up his mountain he went to pray – fervently! I believe he still would have been up there today if the showers of blessing hadn't come. His servant would still be scanning the horizon for the rain cloud with old Elijah exhorting him to *watch* and *pray*! And it came, for the effectual "stretched out" prayer of a righteous man avails much!

What a picture of triumph – followed so soon by defeat! Within a verse or two, Elijah was on the run, fearing for his life. He was threatened not by Ahab and his armies, not by the mighty prophets of Baal and their revengeful families, but frightened out of his mind by a woman. Physically, psychologically and emotionally exhausted, he ran and ran and ran. Finally we find him sitting in the entrance of his cave of disillusionment, his cave of spiritual retirement in his religious mountain.

As I prepared to teach this story in my Bible study, God found me right where I was. I mused in my heart about how exhausted I had been feeling. Many wonderful things were happening. Great congregations. The fire fell week after week: God's life-transforming power evident to the watching people. The prophets of Baal were being defeated. By, oh, how tired I was.

As I climbed my mountain to pray for rain – rivers of living water for the spiritual deserts in men's and women's lives around us – I looked for the rain cloud. It came. God answered prayer every time I prayed, but I was getting far too tired even to climb my mountain. My Christian service was becoming mechanical. Go to the right things, say the right words, look the right way. Answer the same questions, battle with the long phone calls. It was almost a treadmill of Christian activity. I wasn't listening anymore when people spoke to me. I didn't have time to look them straight in the eyes because I was always looking past them, too impatient even to stop for a minute. I was also extremely "remote" at home.

It's at times like this that the snake always produces a Jezebel: someone or some circumstance that takes you under and you find yourself running away. Oh, you can't run away physically, but you surely can mentally. You can withdraw to your cave of retirement, wrap yourself in your cloak of self-pity, and complain religious complaints to the Lord.

"I've been very zealous for you, Lord! I, only I, am left!" How I love the appearance of the Lord Jesus in this story. He knows our frame; he remembers we are dust. When Elijah fell, his face in the ground, totally spent, the angel of the *Lord* (Jesus himself) touched him! He said nothing – no rebuke, no command. He just touched him. Taking his overwrought servant in his arms, loving him, he provided meat and water for his needs. "Let me die," cried Elijah. "I'm no better than my fathers!" Depressed to the point of suicidal contemplations, Elijah longed to be finished with it all.

Now from God's viewpoint, this little incident must have been most frustrating. His plans had been upset. One day away from following through and finishing off Jezebel, Elijah runs away! Israel, thoroughly convinced by the miracle on Carmel, was ready for his leadership. How grateful we should be that God is never peeved and never deals with us as we most certainly would if *we* were God. He simply touched Elijah and patiently waited in the inner recesses of the cave to speak to his exhausted prophet.

In my exhausted state, I found I could be still and experience that "underneath and all around are the everlasting arms." God is in no hurry. We are not indispensable to his plans and purposes. He can wait. And he does. "Beware of the barrenness of a busy life," some-one has said. Sometimes we are sick simply to make us learn to "rest", not only physically, but spiritually.

Once God in his goodness has given us a physical break, it's time for some company. None of us are enti-tled to retirement in some cosy cave where we can put up our feet on an easy rock forever. A cave in the coun-try is no answer to our problem! There are far too many permanent Christian cave dwellers today!

Are you a Christian cave dweller? Are you living in a cave of disillusionment? Upset with God because Jezebel reigns in your kingdom and God just doesn't seem to be cutting loose? Have you lost your faith? Or is it a cave of self-righteousness? "I, only I, am left to care in my church fellowship," you say. Or is it a cave of self-preservation? "They seek my life to take it away!"

I suppose I have spent time in all these and many more caves in my Christian life. But when I've had my rest and licked my wounds and grumbled at God, my cave insulation is never adequate enough to stop the "still small voice".

"What are you doing here, Elijah? This is not the position for you. Go! Return!" You can wrap your ears in your mantle like Elijah did to shut out the voice, but you'll never succeed. The only time you will be allowed to retire is to your heavenly mansion!

Thoroughly exhausted, physically and in every other way, I was busy settling into a cave of self-complacency. The women's retreats were growing, and it gave me a nice swell of pride (which, incidentally, I hastened to call spiritual satisfaction!) to humbly tell of the growth of the work at conventions far and near. Surely

Milwaukee must feel the impact of 2,000 women. I had a vague warning feeling about that smug statement, but being too tired to pray, I dismissed it with a careless shrug.

Walking into church the next Sunday, one of our ushers pushed a little note into my hand. It said simply, "Can you take a ladies' meeting at 9.00 pm next Sunday?" I nodded and went to my seat. The following week as I walked into the service, I hissed at the man who had given me the note, "Where is the meeting?" He scribbled down an address which I didn't even bother to look at.

That evening the snow began to fall as if it intended to get the whole of winter over in one night! The children were more awkward than usual, and we were late for church. We had loaned one of our cars to some missionaries, and they had gotten stuck somewhere. Because I hadn't had time to get ready, I offered to drive my husband and the family to the service and then return home to prepare. My hair was a mess, so I hastily stuck a large hairpiece on my head and hurried outside to the car. Arriving at church to pick up our associate pastor's wife, Gail, I skidded down the entrance slope and the car turned the wrong way around, right in the path of all the cars in the car park. By now the service was well underway. It was blowing a gale, and there was nothing to do but to try and shovel my way out. As I was hardly dressed for such activity, the inevitable happened! A gust of wind, and I was left clutching my lovely hairpiece in one hand and my snow shovel in the other! I had half an hour to go before my meeting, and I had quite a drive to get there!

Tiptoeing into church, I managed to grab Gail, and we made our getaway. She tried to stick my hair back on as I drove, and she managed to produce a rather "chic" over-the-right-ear hairstyle!

"Where are we going?" she inquired.

Suddenly I noticed the snake all dressed up in his Sunday best sitting in the back seat. He was sniggering horribly, and I had a feeling he definitely knew something I didn't know.

All I had was the address. I had no way of knowing whether it was a church gathering, teen meeting, or what! Eventually we arrived. I looked carefully at the address again. Yes, it was right! We had arrived at the local bowling alley! The snake was already at the door eager to get a drink and try his hand. We entered and asked the man if he had seen any group of ladies around.

"Yes," he replied. "They are through that room in the back."

"Gail, I must look a freak!" I muttered. We were too late to care and headed for the back room. The door opened and we went in. Sure enough, there they were. It was a social club, and the first item on the agenda was a wine-tasting experience! The snake was completely at home, thoroughly enjoying the whole situation. Gail and I sat at the back politely allowing the different bottles to pass us by. One thing comforted me: they wouldn't notice my hair! But what on earth was I going to say? No one took any notice of us. Maybe I was in the wrong place, I thought hopefully.

After quite a while, a little man got up and said, "Now then, I see our speaker has arrived. I'm afraid I don't know anything about her." He stopped and suddenly appeared to remember something. "Oh, yes, I do," he countered. "I think she's got a comedy act!" The snake was writhing around in hysterics. As I walked to the front, my mind a complete blank, the gentleman who had introduced me placed a nearly empty bottle of wine in my hand. "It shall be given you in the same hour what ye shall speak," the Lord had said. Fortunately, it was!

"Oh dear," I said, "the wine has run out. That happened once before in a little village called Cana. A marriage started out on the wrong foot. Christ was there at the wedding, but he wasn't the governor. He was only a guest, so the wine ran out and the whole party became flat and dull and insipid. Folks, I've come to talk to you about Christian marriage!"

There was a completely divided audience that night. Some were embarrassed and annoyed; a few were indifferent. But, oh, how many hungry faces turned toward me. And suddenly I realised I'd been on my religious mountain far too long. The cave of self-complacency needed to be left behind, and I needed to obey the still, small voice: "What are you doing here, Eliijah? ... Go back the way you came" – get out where the action is and reach suburban women in America.

"But how, Lord?"

"Don't you remember?" the Lord reminded me. "Start where you are with what you've got. Use the ladies to reach them. Go where they are; don't expect them to come to you."

Well, where were they? In clubs! That's where they were. But how to get in? The snake reminded me that secular clubs jealously guarded their immunity from "religious" speakers.

"There must be a way in, Lord. Show us," I prayed. We began to copy and file a list of every club in Milwaukee. We would start and visit them with a team of two and ask for permission to tell about the forthcoming women's retreat and to testify to what God had done for us through his Word. Then we would leave a brochure with the women offering them East and Christmas programmes. Then – well – then we'd see! The Christmas and Easter readings we would use could be done by two women with or without music or could be dramatised by a small team. The committee got to work drafting the letter.

Out of my cave and back in the world, I thanked God for my "wine-tasting" experience. At the time of this writing, the letters were on the way to their destinations, and we're climbing our mountains to pray for rain. Rain for a spiritually dry country; rain for thirsty people; life-giving rain for the dying.

I believe one day we'll see a cloud, no bigger than a man's hand, and then we'll know the showers of blessing will be well on their way!

19

Changing My Husband

ow that you've had a chance to settle down and live together for a little while, don't you think it's time you started to change your husband?" inquired the snake one day. It so happened that I'd been particularly irritated by one or two little things that morning, so I was far too willing to be drawn into a conversation with the nasty thing. I forgot Eve's lasting example and engaged in a dialogue with the enemy. "Don't you think he ought to be more organised?" the snake inquired.

"Like me?" I asked proudly.

"Yes, dear, just like you!" he replied.

Yes, I did think this would really help matters. If only I could get Stuart to change, to do things my way instead of seemingly at the last minute. The snake knew that Stuart and I were scheduled to speak at a seminar on marriage that afternoon, and I began to get increasingly uptight. My husband had still not told me what he wanted me to do for my part of the meeting.

He certainly hadn't deliberately withheld the information (as the snake was trying to suggest), but for many good reasons he'd just been too hectically busy to get around to telling me.

"Tell him it's time he got prepared," the snake hissed, and before I could stop it, it was out! I received a justified sharp rebuke and in a subdued mood got into the car to go to our seminar on "marriage"!

Things were very quiet in the vehicle (except for that horrid creature chattering in the back seat). I thought hard about it all. Should a wife try to change her husband? Maybe I should change! No, I don't mean change to do everything his way. I don't work like that; but I could certainly take a good look at my partner and, instead of bugging him, seek to help him get things done.

I noted that Stuart usually got things finished, even if some were accomplished at the last minute. The reason for this was that he was trying to do the work of three people. So, I concluded, why couldn't I just schedule *my* time to enable me to be around at these last minutes. To be available – to think ahead for him. I'd try it!

After the silence in the car had continued long enough, we began to laugh. After all, something had to be done. However could we stand up in front of all these people and talk with authority on married bliss! I thought how typical of the snake this was. He was forever slithering around our calendars noting the meetings we had and planning lots of nasty upsetting "happenings" just before we went out the door! Why didn't I see the danger signs? I'd really been on my guard every Thursday morning before my ladies' Bible class for many weeks. Invariably the children would be quite difficult, and I would shout at them or do something that would really give the snake the chance to point his tail. I'd recognised the danger and had been on my guard – so much so that the children were always happy about Thursday mornings. They reckoned they could get away with anything because they knew I couldn't shout at them! But bless them, they didn't push me too hard. They knew the meeting ended at 11.00 am!

The pattern was there. Before any service for the Lord the snake would be busy seeking to wreck relationships. Sitting in the car on the way to our seminar on Christian marriage, I thought about Ephesians 5. I had such a nice scripturally pat talk on submission. It sounded so right, and it was! Straight from the Word. But could I be honest? Honesty was tough for me. The person I had been before my conversion had taken 20 years to submit to his Spirit. When I was first saved and was asked a question I couldn't answer, I just made it up! Lies! Hypocrisy!

I thought about Ananias and Sapphira. "We've given everything," they said. They had consented together to lie. Their joint commitment was complete. God, the God of Truth, knew better. Their witness impressed no one! They were buried along with their lies. Sure, the early Christian church remembered these two. They remembered them for their dishonesty.

I knew we had to be honest, share our problems and his answers. I thought about young John Mark in the Scriptures. What a well-meaning failure he was. Many scholars believe that John Mark was the young follower of Jesus described in Mark 14:51 who fled naked from the Garden of Gethsemane when Jesus was arrested. He failed to follow his Saviour to the cross. Later he failed Paul and Barnabas on his first missionary trip. And yet he made it spiritually in the end. Why? How? What happened? We aren't told specifically the steps to his full commitment, but we do know Barnabas, Uncle Encouragement, picked him up, and we do know his mother believed in prayer, and we do know Peter, perhaps the greatest influence on that young man's life, was honest with him. Mark's Gospel has sometimes been called the Gospel of Peter; i.e. Peter is believed to be the source of the information written there, and I think I know what happened to young John Mark. I think when Peter entrusted him with his stories of Jesus' life, Mark found tremendous encouragement to go on and find victory.

How thankful I am for the people in my life who have been honest enough to be honest! I remembered giving my testimony of my struggle to let Stuart be away so much. A young evangelist's wife walked forward at the end of that meeting. (I didn't know until four years later that before she came to that meeting she had decided to take her life.) All she had tried to do and be as an evangelist's wife was, to her, a hopeless failure. The only talks she'd heard had been idealistic "everything's roses with Jesus" talks. Sharing my failures as well as my victories had been God's answer to that woman's needs.

Stuart and I had a great meeting at our marriage seminar that day. It paved the way for a youth seminar on "Love, Courtship and Marriage" which we were asked to do for thousands of British teens at Spre-e 73 in London the next year.

We were learning to work together. Instead of getting uptight and deciding to "change" Stuart, I decided to change *me*, pray a lot, trust him to give me enough time to prepare, and keep a copy of the following verses of Ephesians from the Amplified Bible for my own instruction.

> *However, let each man of you (without exception) love his wife as [being in a sense] his very own self; and let the wife see that she respects* **and** *reverences her husband – that she notices him, regards him, honours him, prefers him, venerates and esteems him; and that she defers to him, praises him, and loves and admires him exceedingly. (Ephesians 5:33, AMP)*

After reading this verse in The Amplified Bible, I looked at my dictionary just to make sure I understood what reverence really meant.

1. *Notice him* – heed; pay attention to. Take delight in your husband. Don't ignore him.
2. *Regard him* – gaze upon with a steady, significant look. Listen to; give full attention. When he comes home, don't chatter endlessly about your day; he may be impatient to get a word in about *his* day.
3. *Honour him* – pay high respect; place in an exalted position. If you expect to be treated like a queen, you must treat him like a king of his castle. Don't put him down.

4. *Prefer him* – promote him; believe in him. Help him to believe in himself.
5. *Venerate and esteem him* – consider worthy, appreciate and prize him. Remember that you picked him, and it doesn't say much for your good taste if you can't venerate and esteem him.
6. *Defer to him* – make concessions in opinions and actions. Be the first to say you're sorry. Is winning your point worth a full-scale row or a "cold war"?
7. *Praise him* – express warm approval. Don't hesitate to tell him. Say it! If you don't, he may listen to another who will.
8. *Love and admire him exceedingly* – love deeply. *Enjoy* your husband!

No man could help loving a woman like that!

20

The Pastor's Children

*A*nd where are your children, Mrs Briscoe?" asked a lady visiting our church. "Oh, they're around," I answered casually.

I didn't want to point them out. Not because I was ashamed of them, but because I didn't want them to be objects of curiosity ... different ... "the pastor's kids". P.K.'s are supposed to be a special race. The wild ones! The kids who always fall off pedestals they never mounted. We wanted to shield them from this kind of pressure.

However, we tried to give our children a sense of pride and privilege in being part of a family whose vocation is to serve. And this they appeared to understand and accept without reluctance. Ever since our earliest days at Capernwray in England, the children had grown up with a sense of mission. Our home was certainly our home, but its doors were always open; its rooms, however small, were always full – and they loved it. If, for a moment of time, no visitor or "adopted" family member would be living with us, our eldest boy would soon be asking, "Who's coming next? No visitors for lunch?" Of course, they benefited, too. What a blessing our constant stream of visitors have been to our little ones.

One student from Germany began to do David's Bible reading with him. She was concerned about his bedtime story inevitably being cut short by an important phone call or some minor or major crisis connected with the teenage youth work for which I was responsible. Purchasing some Scripture Union notes at his age level, she so instilled a disciplined habit of Scripture reading into him that he can look back to seven years of nightly study. How grateful we are to that young woman.

Sometimes the children have seen broken, marred lives enter our home. They have watched God's transforming power begin to work. They have also learned the crippling lessons of human beings refusing to allow healing and have watched the resultant disintegration of a marriage situation or life itself.

How grateful I was to my Lord for giving us these precious teen years together with our children. We knew that the church life would be an important part of the help we would need. And I was well aware that God would be using others to be a blessing to our children in their teen years, even as we had managed to help other people's children.

Praying about my part as their mother, I decided I would work in their age group in the church programme, and I was able to begin the junior high work. We began with eleven children. I discovered they loved to pray. The first time was a bit dramatic – for them and me. I handed a Bible to the first boy and said, "OK, kids, we are all going to pray aloud. When someone hands you the Bible, start praying!" Then I quickly shut my eyes, but not before I'd glimpsed their horrified faces! Everyone prayed! The next time was better, and the third meeting we no longer needed to pass the Bible.

We started simple Bible studies, interaction groups, using different creative approaches, mixed with a little fun and recreation. The young people loved it, and soon we were having testimony nights and five-minute talks on different topics, music nights, poetry, art and drama presentations, and anything else that would help us all get to know the Lord better and encourage full participation from the youngsters. The small inter-action groups helped us find out their spiritual needs, and we discovered that a lot of the printed junior high material was written to cure chicken pox when it was a case of measles that needed treating.

We began a question box, answering a few each week. "What's prematerial sex?" (He meant premarital!) "Now I'm a Christian, can I kiss a girl?" asked a bright thirteen-year-old boy. "What's hell like?" asked another. "Well, I guess hell is like being able to take one good look at God and then never being allowed to look again," answered another.

The time was always lively and interesting, and it was a great thrill to me to have my two young teens in that group of eager learners. I found I had severely underestimated their capacity for understanding the Bible. Many of them began to study the Navigator material or used Scripture Union daily readings. They learned how to do book reviews to share with the group.

Bible study materials produced for grammar school or even university students were handled well by a bright minority. Our own twelve-year-old daughter took a file to church and made excellent sermon outlines. How thrilling to be my children's spiritual and physical mother! I had led Peter and Judy to Christ when they were very young. Now I could give them principles to build their lives upon in the vital years. Precept upon precept, line upon line, here a little, there a little.

Peer pressure is a great influence in their early teens, and I realised it was up to me – especially in the summer months – to have "open house" all the time, to provide barbecues and swimming fun, games and sleepovers, inviting many of our children's Christian friends into our home circle. It's true that you can't choose your children's friends, but there are many practical ways you can surround them with Christian youngsters so they are more likely to choose their closest friends from a Christian group.

I found myself beginning to live on my knees! I asked the Holy Spirit to tell me when one of the children needed prayer. Perhaps a vulnerable moment at school, a moral danger, a physical need. Over and over again an inner "bug" would tell me to pray, and then the peace came. I knew I would have to get to heaven before I would find out all the miracle answers to those prayers. I prayed that each child would not just be "good" – you know, have enough religion to make him or her respectable. I prayed for a fully committed young life as early as possible: fullness of life, wholeness of personhood, usability by God, and a life fully set aside and sold out for him, whether in secular society or full-time Christian service. I knew this had to be the best thing I could ever wish for my children.

Into my busy schedule I included some specific time when I would do "something" with each child individually. Singling them out was a real relationship-building experience. I asked each of the older children to take turns having Peter's quiet time with him and also helped to organise outreach for them at their own level.

Little teams, consisting of our children and their friends, began to be formed from their group to go to nursing homes, orphanages, disabled centres and small Bible schools. They would write down their skills, and then we would team them up and send them forth. Some could sing or play an instrument. Some said they wanted to talk or witness. One told us he was an excellent juggler, while another could draw while someone preached!

Our children had so much head knowledge of the Scriptures, but I knew it would only be applied as they verbalised it and tried to share it with others.

I experienced many fears and discovered that "fear hath torment". The Bible also says that God hasn't given us the spirit of fear. If God hadn't given it to us, then I knew the source. The snake! He made sure I experienced reasonable and unreasonable fear, and the only relief I found were the promises of God and perfect love, and both were rediscovered on my knees. "Perfect love casts out fear." It was on my knees that I remembered he loved my children more than I could ever love them. What was more, he reminded me I hadn't saved them; therefore I didn't have to keep them! He kept those he chose, and no one would be able to tear them from his grasp! I began to pray specifically as problems arose and see specific answers to prayer.

Our children's spare time was completely wrapped up in the life of the church. By choice, too. How my heart thrilled as David, at fifteen, was able to go on tour with a Christian musical group. They sang and witnessed, prayed and shared. They were opened up to his Spirit to take over their young lives.

When one of the children had a period of struggle, I began to share the need with a few "real pray-ers". The results were so thrilling and encouraging. We shared some of our burdens about the church and prayed daily around the meal table for people and situations, church and school problems.

I suddenly realised that these years were precious years of opportunity – soon to be gone – when we could enjoy and know our children as *people*. I asked the Lord that I would have no regrets looking back when they were over. And I prayed that looking forward with his omniscient power he would have no regrets either where our precious children's lives were concerned.

I love Amy Carmichael's poem about her "children". I pray it often. Amy worked among the children of India, rescuing them from the fate of prostitution in the heathen temples. Sometimes her children were stolen from the mission compound. Then she could only pray:

Father, hear us, we are praying,
Hear the words our hearts are saying,
We are praying for our children.

Keep them from the powers of evil,
From the secret, hidden peril,
Father, hear us for our children.

From the whirlpool that would suck them,
From the treacherous quicksand, pluck them,
Father, hear us for our children.

From the worldling's hollow gladness,
From the sting of faithless sadness,
Father, Father, keep our children.

Through life's troubled waters steer them,
Through life's bitter battles cheer them,
Father, Father, be Thou near them.

Read the language of our longing,
Read the wordless pleadings thronging,
Holy Father, for our children.

And wherever they may bide,
Lead them Home at eventide.

21

Walkie-Talkie

In all our relationships there is a choice set before us. We can do our "duty" or we can identify. With our children we can do those things mothers do: wash their clothes, fill their stomachs and choose the best schools for their education. I heard a lady give her testimony once, and she started off by saying, "I was a good mother to my children – but, then, so was my cat!" We can "buy" them fun; especially in America. I found much "fun" on the market. Legitimate healthy sport and exercise, and club life. We can give them everything – except ourselves!

We are too impatient to identify. And it's only when we identify that we can communicate. So many people live in the same house and play "walkie-talkie"! Our two boys loved to play walkie-talkie. Somebody had given them two little radio sets, and they would make sure they never came into contact. Then they would speak a cryptic message into the receiver. Just a word or two. Nothing important, just enough to let the other know they were in the house. Then a little phrase would come over the air, "Over and out!"

How many of us are playing walkie-talkie with someone we live with? Maybe we don't even realise we are doing it. We get into a remote position in a relationship and every now and then throw out a little phrase to make sure the other hears our voice – and then it's "over and out" without meaningful communication ever happening. We tuck our children up in bed and they cling to us, asking irrelevant questions, giving us news that really is not at all related to our adult world. "They're just putting off the 'sleep' hour," we say impatiently as we pat them, kiss them, tuck them up and tell them, "No, you can't have another glass of water!"

There came a time in my experience when I stopped being impatient inside; I got that second glass of water and brought it to my child, sprawled on her bed, and began to identify. I got inside her life; I listened to her hopes, her fears, bit my tongue when she'd tell me things I wanted to "moralise" about and sought to show her "why not to" instead of responding with a "you're not to". The visitors could wait. The phone call could be made later. *Nothing* mattered in that moment of time except my little girl. And I asked myself what I'd been doing all these years!

Could my children be free to tell me how they'd failed? They were the pastor's kids. They weren't supposed to fail. If they did, would I be the one they'd tell so I could assure them that failure made no difference to love? They wouldn't confide in me if I'd been playing "walkie-talkie"!

What about the "boy-girl" bit? How could my son like that little blonde who obviously wasn't going to be good for him instead of that cute red-haired deacon's child? The temptation to tell him he had to like who I liked was intense! Were he and I identifying enough to have him share his relationships with me – not ask me my opinion, but tell me his feelings, his fears and hopes. And if he wasn't asking me, I learned I wasn't to tell him. I needed to listen, pray, commit it, and let him know that *when* he got around to asking he'd get an unbiased opinion based on the principles of the Word of God, instead of an overprotective rose-tinted mother's angle on the issue!

And what about other relatives? What about my mother-in-law? Well, now, everyone knows we need to identify with our family, but no one expects us to do anything *but* play "walkie-talkie" with mother-in-law! After all, didn't the Bible say we were to "leave" our parents and cleave to our husbands? Some people take that verse as their biblical excuse for abandoning all responsibility. In fact, some women have a warmer relationship with the girl at the supermarket counter than they ever do with their own husband's mother!

Having one of the most beautiful, warm relationships with my own wonderful mother certainly made me desire a similar experience with Stuart's mother. Obviously it could never be the same, but I realised right from the start the quality of our times together was of great importance.

The snake's campaigns to wreak havoc with this "special" relationship are so successful that I refuse even to give him mention in this chapter. Suffice it to say, he is very busy and usually very successful!

Visits of in-laws are usually confined to special holidays, etc., depending on distance separating the "combatants". No, don't think that's too strong a word. After being in the pastorate and being involved in many family situations, that is the only way I can describe some of these relationships! But what about a situation that necessitates longer visits? Well, you can sit around and hope it doesn't happen to you, decide that can only work out if you are an unusual sort of person, or take a good hard look at yourself and ask the Lord just what he expects our attitude to be.

When we invited my mother-in-law to visit us for a three-month stay, I decided I needed to do just that. Where was I to look? Well, it would help if there was actually an example of a mother-in-law/daughter-in-law situation right in the Scriptures. I found the obvious one and settled down to study it. It was, of course, in the book of Ruth. Actually it is the story of a contrasted relationship: Orpah and Ruth both having the same mother-in-law and both women having the same choice. They could identify or play "walkie-talkie".

Naomi had done a good job. For her part, she had been able to accept and love the two heathen girls her sons had chosen as their wives – girls who were different from herself. Her witness and her love had been enough to convert Ruth to the Lord Jehovah. Orpah, too, loved her mother-in-law and started out with Ruth to accompany her back to her homeland. Tragedy had struck the family and death had visited their home taking away all of their menfolk. Now they would seek a new life together in Naomi's homeland.

On the way home, Naomi stopped and, apparently feeling it was a selfish thing to take the girls with her, gave them another chance to choose. "You go your way; I'll go mine. Our customs and ways and even our gods and the way we worship are so different. I cannot take you with me. We could never live together. There would be too many problems and conflicts." Somewhere along the road we, too, have to choose. We can go our separate ways or we can go on together. We can *try* or we can *tolerate*.

Now the crunch came. Orpah wept, kissed her mother-in-law, and left. Each agreed quite amicably to go her own way. They would play "walkie-talkie". But Ruth! She clung to Naomi and said, "Don't urge me to leave you or turn back from you. Where you go I will go, and where you stay I will stay. Your people will be my people and your God my God. Where you die I will die, and there I will be buried. May the LORD deal with me, be it ever so severely, if anything but death separates you and me" (Ruth 1:16–17). In effect Ruth said, "I'm going to *identify*!" A kiss is not enough if we profess to be Christians. Ruth was *determined* to go with Naomi. She simply made up her mind about the matter.

There it was. I could be an Orpah or a Ruth. Mine was the choice. I had the strangest sense of immense importance as I read these words. It's a bit dramatic, I thought. After all, Mum is only coming for a three-month visit. I told the Lord I wanted to be a Ruth, not an Orpah. I saw how Ruth had honoured Naomi, shared her joys and fears with her. She had placed her child within her arms to love and cherish. I realised how Naomi had surrendered her right to have Boaz for herself. "Submit yourself one to the other" was not written for husbands and wives alone!

Mother came, and we had a great time. Four weeks after her arrival, I had to take her to the hospital, only to discover that she had cancer! Three operations and nine months later, I was thinking about the lessons of that book. Of one thing I'm sure – the only way is a "daily" Ruth identification. The daily choice is ours. I made it and I wanted it, and so did Naomi. Orpah wept and returned to her own country, her own kin, and her own selfishness. Ruth married Boaz. She became the richest woman in town, having a part in the line of the Lord Jesus Christ himself. To be a Ruth means inevitable relationship with Jesus Christ, and in the end that is *all* that matters.

I love the story of Ruth. It records for us the story of Naomi and Ruth's homecoming. It says the whole city was stirred because of them. On her own confession, Naomi had gone away full; now she returned empty, except for the precious gift of the love of her daughter-in-law.

You may read this and say, "Well, I'm not as lucky as you. My mother-in-law is no Naomi!" The Bible points out that Naomi was a lonely, bitter woman. "Call me Mara," she said. "Mara" means "bitterness". Love changed all that – Ruth's overflowing love. She trusted her child into Naomi's care. She respected her advice. She never returned empty-handed at the end of the day. All that she had gathered that day she shared. She just decided to try and share her blessings. No wonder the whole city was moved.

Boaz, in testimony to Ruth, told her how people had spoken to him about all that she had done for her mother-in-law. "God will bless you for it," he said. And, of course, he always does.

Do you want to move a city? Don't plan an evangelistic campaign. Try being a Ruth!

22

God Can

Who can turn stones into children? God can! Yes, he can! The Bible says it, or to be more accurate, John the Baptist said it to the Pharisees who were so proud of being Abraham's sons by birth that they had forgotten to be like their *Father* in character. It's no big deal, said John, "I tell you that out of these stones God can raise up children for Abraham" (Matthew 3:9).

I was having my quiet time and thoroughly enjoying my thoughts. "God can, God can, God can," I repeated over and over again. "God can even turn stones into children!"

Suddenly I heard the snake. I couldn't quite see where he was because he always keeps his distance when he sees us reading the Bible, which, of course, he hates, twists, distorts and ridicules. But even from a distance I could distinctly hear him hiss, "Of course God can do anything (or so he says). So if he can turn stones into children, he can presumably turn children into stones as well." My heart beat a little faster. He had my full attention. Dave, Judy and Pete had raced into the turbulent teens, banners flying, eyes wide with joy – determined to live life to the full, dragging their reluctant mother screaming and kicking along with them.

"Don't be intimidated," advised a good friend (whose children were already married).

"Face these years as a challenge to your faith," suggested another (who didn't have any children at all).

"Trust the Lord. He *can* keep them safe," contributed yet another (whose children were a real mess) somewhat doubtfully. All their well-meant counsel didn't really help.

"Oh, yes," chortled the snake, enjoying himself, "God can turn children into stones!"

Reason prevailed. "But *God* wouldn't do that," I objected. "Why should he? He wants all to repent and come to him. He constantly works by his Spirit convicting people of sin, convincing them that Jesus is the answer, and converting them to himself. So why would *he* turn *my* children into hard, obdurate little rebels? "No (I warmed to my theme), he wouldn't," (then I had a flash of insight) "but *you* would!"

Now the snake didn't like that at all. He hates to have his suggestive ideas examined by the light of the principles of Scripture. He wants us to live in a constant fear mode, ever waiting for the worst to happen. But even though there was quiet in my soul for a little while at least, some persistent troubling thoughts remained.

"God *could* make children out of stones; that was not in question," I mused as I went about my duties of the day. "But the little things had free will that I *could* do nothing about, and God *would* do nothing about, or he wouldn't have given it them in the first place. *And* then there was a snake in their gardens." That was the most scary thought of all! If I didn't recognise the creature so much of the time, however would they see his diabolical shape?

He was back again, this time with a photo album he wanted to show me. He had been busy developing the pictures in the nether regions (they were actually still wet), but I could see he had duplicated a very good likeness of my three children. They resembled them enough to give me a horrible, sick feeling in the pit of my stomach. The pictures were many: Dave, flunking out of school, working in the sewer system; Judy pregnant at fifteen; Pete in a wheelchair at seventeen, having been paralysed from the neck down playing football!

"But," I almost shouted, dragging my eyes away from the images, *"God can."*

"Ah, but *will he?*" interrupted the snake. "Will he? *That's* the question!"

And that *was* the question. I knew and the snake knew that God *can* do anything. But the "will he do it?" was the thing. And what would happen when his will met their will head on? Who would win? I didn't know, and I began to worry and fret the weeks away, waiting for disaster. "Lord, if only you would lean out of heaven and just tell me it's all right, I'd be a lot more relaxed," I prayed. "Why I might even be able to enjoy these years!"

"But you're so brave," the snake said smoothly. "Ssssoooo brave. It's just as well though," he added chillingly, "because you're going to need to be very, very brave – *very*, soon."

There it was again. What did he mean? What was going to happen soon? I wondered. It was just as if every day was spoiled before it even began, because I was waiting to be "very brave" when I needed to be – preparing for the *worst* while in actuality the *best* was happening!

The children were really in great shape. Sure they were being normal thirteen-, fifteen-, and seventeen-year-olds, but God was indeed active in all of their lives. The disasters I had been anticipating were not materialising, and I began to realise they might not!

That was a big step for me away from the "might" to the "might not". In fact, that realisation made the snake tie himself in two knots! "Just wait!" he screeched, "just wait…"

"But those who wait for the Lord (not for the disaster) shall renew their strength. They will soar on wings like eagles; they will run and not grow weary, they will walk and not be faint," Omnipotence reminded me. "You can *wait* for me to renew and revitalise you *and* your children, or you can spend your waking moments waiting for the enemy to make good his threats. And remember," he added, "he is the created one, but I am the Creator. He isn't God – I am, and beside me there is no other." With that eternal reminder, he began to pour into my worried soul soothing promises about his love and perfect ability to "guard what I have entrusted to him for that day" (2 Timothy 1:12). "You weep; I'll keep," he said. In effect, "Cry if you will, but it's very unnecessary." Now I began to even dare to enjoy those dreaded teenage years!

All this time my husband was having a great time. It was just as if he'd been waiting forever for the children to grow up and play with him. What a father he was, and oh, how we all revelled in having him around and part of the action. And action there was. He wasn't intimidated by it all, that was for sure. The children responded to his positive reinforcement. When the snake would suggest that being a P.K. was the most unfair life sentence in the world, Stuart would be busy telling them there were certain unavoidable things that went with the territory – certain expectations they couldn't escape. There were behaviour patterns that were doubly fitting for children privileged to belong to leaders of the flock. But along with what might seem to them to be these minor drawbacks, God had been gracious enough to give them a view on life in a kingdom *only* visible from the parsonage. The snake's voice faded, drowned out by such happy, affirming talk. "Yes, it may be a pain to *have* to go to church three times instead of two like most of your friends," Stuart commented one day, catching a gripe on the subject before it developed any further, "but that's how it is when you're a pastor's child." Church really wasn't an issue until – yes, there was *one* "until".

It happened shortly after Pete's thirteenth birthday. Apparently, the snake had been telling him he knew as much, or even a little bit more, than his Sunday School teacher. So why bother to do anything but quit that useless activity? Pete graduated himself! Then I discovered the reptile had been making large posters with the word "boring" all over them and placing them in strategic positions. The snake even wrapped Pete's Bible in one, stuck one on the church door, and even hung one over his dad's head while he was preaching. (There's no end to his arrogance!)

One day we had a guest speaker, a good friend, staying at our house. My husband had left early in order to get things ready at the church, and I was rounding up the children to follow him. I duly corralled Dave and Judy who were more or less ready, but when I looked for Pete, he was nowhere to be found. "Pete!" I shouted. "Where are you? We're late!" Looking up the stairs my eyes met the big brown eyes of my youngest son, usually alive with dancing lights, but now still and sombre.

"I'm not coming!" he announced with finality. At once I saw the snake curled up by his side, nodding approvingly and smirking. I saw he had propped a cushion behind Pete's head. Pete was exhausted after an exciting game of basketball and had flicked open the TV guide to the Sunday sports programme. The snake also had a set of cue cards in his hands.

"Pete," I said with some sense of trepidation, "hurry up. Don't be silly; you're making our guest speaker late." I was embarrassed because the said guest speaker was standing there listening in on the conversation. I needn't have worried about his feelings, however, as he was killing himself laughing out of sight around the corner in the kitchen! Well, that didn't help. *Why didn't he come to my aid?* I wondered.

"Pete," he said, responding to my somewhat desperate look, "come on. Your dad and I are going to have some fun introducing each other tonight. He's going to introduce me, but I'm going to get my chance to introduce him first!"

Pete respected our friend and loved the joking that went on between him and his dad, but he answered in all seriousness, "Sir, my dad doesn't need an introduction, he needs a conclusion!"

Well! The guest speaker thought that was really funny, and the snake couldn't believe he hadn't even had to use one cue card. Pete was doing very well all by himself. I did notice, however, the customary "boring" sign was hanging (crooked, of course) on the wall just above Pete's head where it would be sure to catch his eye.

Exerting all the influence I could, I "commanded" Pete to get in the car just as he was as there was no time left to change. (Thereby taking away that excuse before he thought of it.)

"He can't go to God's house looking like that," screeched the snake (who had *already* thought of it). "Why, the Holy Spirit," he choked on the word, "won't let him in the door."

But to my great surprise, Pete did what he was told, and off we went to worship. Fat chance of that, I thought grimly. How can you worship when you've come straight from World War II in your kitchen? On getting into the church lobby, Pete disappeared behind the coatracks, and I headed in after him.

It didn't help to hear Judy's amazed comment to David. "Do you mean we could have rebelled, too?" How glad I was the idea had apparently not occurred to her until now!

Yes, we had had our moments with the older ones, but the issue of church attendance had not been one of them – until that day. I was fleetingly so grateful for Dave – stable, sure, right-on Dave. Our first child.

Always so steady, loving the Lord, showing the way, lighting the path, being the example I needed at the "top" of the family.

Behind the coatracks I eventually found Pete. "Pete," I said as quietly as I could, aware of people averting their eyes as they left their outerwear on hangers and hurried away, thinking goodness knows what, having discovered the pastor's wife confronting her youngest, tallest, angriest and "hardest" challenge. God can, God can, God can make children out of stones, I was reminding myself breathlessly, trying not to listen to the snake saying at the same time, "But with their cooperation, I can make stones out of children."

"Pete, please listen to me," I insisted.

I talked, wrestled, pleaded, prayed, argued, cajoled, commanded, threatened, and something paid off and Pete left the sanctity of the coatracks, dragging himself at floor height into the pew. Once more the groups of people in the lobby kindly averted their eyes and kept on talking, though I was searingly aware that not one was missing the drama. "Pete doesn't want to go to church," announced a loud voice. It was the snake with a horrible bullhorn (interestingly, though not at all surprisingly, actually in the shape of a horn)!

"I'm praying for Pete," murmured a lady out of the corner of her mouth.

"And for you," whispered her companion.

"Thank you very much," I muttered, hurrying by as the first hymn greeted me: "Onward, Christian soldier, marching as to war!" Well, that's something I can relate to, I thought, grimly taking my seat.

So began some long hard months for me when Pete sat with his head on his hands throughout the church service, and I struggled to care more about my young son's ambivalence than about what the church people would think of *me*, their senior pastor's wife! "Teenagers are so *visible*," I complained to my husband. My daughter suggested I sit behind a pillar so I couldn't see what they were doing, and my eldest suggested Pete take a book to church if he was bored.

I rejected both "meant-to-be-helpful" comments by pointing out our services were lively and interesting, and that their dad was known to be one of the best preachers in the world. There was no argument from them. They knew it as best they could know it, but their interest was tempered with huge issues of their own, and the day had not yet come when they would appreciate Elmbrook with all its rich resources.

A comment from a sermon changed my focus. "You've got to forgive your child for being thirteen," the speaker was saying. I didn't hear the rest of her talk! That's what I needed to hear, and that's what I needed to do. I had to recognise and accept the fact that Pete was only being what he was, a perfectly normal thirteen-year-old. He was finding his faith, wasn't really rebellious – not enough to sneak around – was far too nice a child to be anything worse than bored and show it. A great wave of concern and love came over me. This was my baby, the last of the crew, our joy, our lively, lovely, funny, creative, crazy, youngest one.

As I would say at his wedding (but oh, how far off that day seemed then) he was, "easy to raise, easy to praise, and so easy to love." I was to lose him for a while as all of us parents will as our children learn the hard and sometimes cruel lessons of adolescence, but I would receive him back again as a vibrant, strong, committed junior high youth pastor of all things! And more, Pete would become an outstanding young minister of the Gospel of the Jesus he and I loved with our whole hearts. If only I had known that *then*. But I didn't. I couldn't. I could only go on a step at a time, forgiving him for being thirteen, then fourteen, fifteen, sixteen, and on until he became my friend again. Omnipotence kissed my fears away and sent me on my way, back into my world of parenting a few inches taller in Jesus than I had been before.

"God can, God can, God can turn stones into children," I whispered to Omnipotence.

He smiled at me, and I'm sure I heard him answer, "And I *will*."

23

Needing to Be Needed

avid was coming home! I was so excited I couldn't stand it. After six long months we would get to see him again. It had been a long time – too long. Stuart and I had been in South Africa on a tour of ministry when Dave set off for university.

"What sort of a mother are you?" said a snakey voice, "flying off into the wild blue yonder and letting your poor little lad fend for himself?" The familiar sick feeling of mother guilt crept back again. I thought about it. That wasn't fair. It had been really, really hard being halfway round the big world and not able to pack up our eldest and send him on his way.

"Judy helped," I started to defend myself.

"Judy," the reptile almost spat, interrupting me. "She's only a child – sixteen years of age! Child neglect I call it!"

I thought about my homesick heart far away in

South Africa and comforted myself with the memories of the happy letters I received from Dave and Judy telling me they had managed just fine. In fact, Dave and his little sister had had a big adventure together – Judy "mothering" her brother and helping him get settled. But to come home and face his horribly empty, tidy room that echoed with his absence, which mirrored the feeling in my heart, had not been easy.

Dave, settling into a full university experience, worked hard, played hard, and joined the football team. That had taken care of his holiday times, so now we were left with a precious ten brief days before he left to work down South for the summer.

"Never mind," I comforted myself, "I'll make up for it." And forthwith I began to plan every moment of those few days we were to have together. Stuart did warn me that maybe David would not want to fulfil such a gruelling marathon of family fun and festivities, but I happily ignored him and went ahead anyway. After all, I couldn't imagine why my beloved eldest would not be thrilled to bits with my well-laid plans.

And now his little red car was pulling into the driveway. Judy, Pete and Dad mobbed the door to be first to welcome him. There on the step stood my son, looking good enough to eat, and there by his side – or more accurately "attached" to his side – was the cutest little thing imaginable, already "eating him" with her eyes! "Hi, Mom," Dave greeted me in a somewhat distracted fashion. "Hi Pete, Judy, Dad. This is Amy. She's come to stay for ten days. That's OK, isn't it?"

The snake was mouthing, "NO, IT ISN'T" in my ear, and my heart was shouting it too, so loud I was quite convinced everyone could hear it. Somehow I managed to sputter, "Of course, of course, come on in." Actually, Dave was lost again in two beautiful brown eyes and didn't even notice his mother's valiant efforts to suffocate her reactions. And so began one of the worst ten days of my life! The snake was thoroughly delighted. I found him deliberately tearing up my clever schedule of family plans.

"I don't know *when* you'll *ever* get near him," he commented pleasantly. "Did you see how she even poured his Cornflakes™ into his dish for him while you hovered in the background with your full box of Total™? What a shame," he continued. "I feel sorry for you really; you're sort of a useless old thing, don't you think?"

The problem was, I did think it! I couldn't shake that very feeling: irrelevance. I struggled on. Day after day it seemed to get worse. Judy and Pete said they were disappointed Dave wasn't around more to do some "things" with them. "He's doing 'things' with her, that's why," shrieked the snake with evident relish.

The young woman was a sweet girl. She was a believer and obviously adored Dave. But that was the trouble. I wasn't ready for anyone else to adore him but me. After all, he was only a babe! A mere eighteen years of age, and when the snake pointed out the wedding announcements in the church bulletin, remarking on the youthfulness of those getting married these days, I felt sick.

It wasn't that I didn't try to get through to my son. I tried all right. One day I asked him for his dirty clothes. Suddenly the only thing in the world I *really* wanted to do was his wash! "It's OK, Mum, my girlfriend's done it for me."

"In *your* washing machine," the snake informed me. He was sitting at the kitchen table reading births, MARRIAGES, deaths. (He liked the deaths most, I observed.) "Why don't you check it out? Maybe she didn't know how to work the machine and you can correct her mistake," he added casually.

I have no idea why I allowed myself to be so directed by the horrible creature, but I found myself trotting off downstairs into the basement and actually opening the door of the washing machine and looking inside. What I expected to see, don't ask me, but there it was – his washing – just as Dave had said. What I didn't expect to see was her washing too, with his, all tumbling around together! "It's not decent," screamed the snake, arriving down the drain pile hurriedly to follow up his advantage. "Why don't you say something? Why, they're not even engaged ... yet!"

I climbed the stairs from the laundry room with a heavy heart. What on earth was wrong with me? Why was I having such a terrible battle? I talked it over with my ever-patient husband, who didn't seem to be having a problem at all! "Maybe you're forgetting he's an adult now, Jill," he suggested. "Remember we decided once our children went to university we would let them know we would consider them adults. They don't need to consult us for permission to fall in love, you know."

This whole idea of a "set time" for a change of attitude in parent-child relationship had been an excellent idea for them and for us, for many reasons. To begin with, it helped me to stop asking them where they were going, where they had been, when they would be home, and *who* was on the phone or writing them all those letters. Of course we let them know we didn't expect to have our home treated like a hotel, but we tried to let go of the control.

"That's it," I said, suddenly aware I had hit on something. "Control! I've lost control. That's why I feel so 'unsafe' about all of this." Omnipotence suggested it wasn't a question of losing control but rather giving it to him. That helped me a bit, but I still felt sort of helpless and adrift, like a ship without an anchor. Up to now I'd had such a large part in David's decisions. Now he was making his large choices without me having a part, without inviting my input, and I was scared. And yet, there was something more to it than that.

Omnipotence suggested I "lay it down". "Remember," he told me, "you're not letting the relationship go, just the dependence on the relationship." There now – that rang a bell loud and clear. How many times in my life had I been to this altar? How many times had I been alerted to the need to let go? Now here we were again.

"That's the stupidest thing I've ever heard," the snake sniffed. Actually he really hadn't heard Omnipotence's words at all, as he can't hear them clearly, you know. But he'd caught snatches of that voice that was for him sheer hell to hear, and he had guessed the rest. "I think your son is exceedingly selfish," he offered. "He's not giving a thought to you and your feelings. Why look at him, oblivious to the wonderful meal you've spent hours cooking for him and that pest of a girlfriend. All he does is sit there, smiling that stupid lovesick smile into his meat and potatoes!" It was true. Not the selfishness part, I wouldn't buy that

– I knew my David too well – but the bit about the smile, that was true all right!

The holiday wore on, and each day seemed to be darker and more difficult than the one before. And then it was over. Over without one of my dreams having become reality. They were packing to leave and it was supper time. "Mum, why don't you make us some egg and chips," Dave asked, "like you used to make us back in England?" I couldn't believe it! Dave actually wanted *me, me* to do something for him. I never thought I'd be so happy to see an egg.

"You're not cooking it right," the snake observed, slithering himself on Dave's suitcase standing in the hallway. Whizzing past me at that moment, Dave looked into the pan, saw my eggs bleeding and dying in the pan (like my wounded ego) and commented briefly, "Hey, Mum, do them over easy." Then, seeing my startled look, he said, "Wait a minute." And to my utmost chagrin, called upstairs for "her" to come and show *me* how to do it. The snake fell off the suitcase laughing. I exploded in angry tears and rushed off into our bedroom, out of sight. The snake followed me.

"Poor thing," he said, eyeing me maliciously. "What a thing to say to you. Who does she think she is anyway? What does *she* know about *eggs*? You're quite within your rights to be mad." So saying he got out a fan that he always uses to fan the flames of anger into an infernal inferno!

Dave's face appeared round the door – startled and worried. "Mum, hey, what did I do? What's up?"

"Insensitive boy," cooed the snake. "What's wrong with him? Why can't he see what's up? Fine pastor he'll make! Dumb, I'd call him."

But I didn't know what was up. I only knew I was miserable and worried and had a big hole deep down inside. I hated feeling like this and being like this, but there didn't seem to be one thing I could do about it. "Dave," I sputtered, "I don't know what's wrong with me unless..." and suddenly it was all there as clear as crystal, "unless it's a struggle that most mums go through when they find themselves outside their children's lives looking into a relationship that's out of bounds to them," I said with a flash of inspiration. "I think I need to be needed, and I'm not needed anymore." And then the floodgates really opened! The snake was appalled. He stopped handing me tissues and threw the box at me, disappearing outside.

Dave sat on the bed and with great concern listened to me blubbering on, explaining as best I could what it felt like to bring to birth a child, pour your life into him for eighteen years, and then "step down" and let someone else do it for you, expecting you with not so much as a by your leave to take a back seat! We talked a long time.

"I thought there had to be something more serious than the egg, Mum," Dave said earnestly.

"It's not the egg, but what the egg represents," I sniffed.

Looking suddenly very bewildered, Dave said, "Mother, what *does* the egg represent?" And then we laughed, which as ever proved to be the very best medicine at times like these.

"It's hard, Dave," I whispered. "It's, oh, so hard. I love you so much. This might sound stupid, but it's just hard to see someone else loving you too. It's sort of not my turn anymore!" I think he understood, as much as an eighteen-year-old could. After all, it was just the beginning.

He would have to learn too. Learn to love on his own level. Learn to choose his loves and make room in his relationships for other people, like his family and his friends. Find out how to share his loves with the love-less world, spreading his joy around. There would be more loves before "the love of his life – and ours" came home to us. And there would be more tears – many more – and more traumas and more dramatics from Mother before we were through. But there would be more grace and power to cope as well. More insight gained in handling the task of adapting to having three adults in the family instead of three children and enjoying it. And this was only the beginning. I didn't dare start to think about Judy and Pete. And I didn't need to, Stuart assured me. "Let's take one step at a time," he said. "Yesterday's victories are never intended for today or tomorrow," he reminded me.

I penned a poem then, entitled "I Laid it Down Today." It perfectly described my feelings of worry and fear, and my need to turn the weight of those feelings over to the Lord. It reminded me that in order to walk by faith, I must lay down my need to be needed.

That night I laid out some special family pictures on my bed and after a long, long look I again read the poem and tried to make the essence of it my prayer.

Omnipotence smiled. I know he heard me! And over the years, I can tell you, he answered me!

24

Famous for What?

"You're famous," said the snake admiringly. "I know," I replied modestly. After all, I had walked into the big convention and had heard a group of women behind me whisper, "There's Jill Briscoe."

"Doesn't that make you feel good?" said the snake smoothly, holding a big mirror right in front of my face while he balanced a halo over my head. I noticed the halo was a little cracked and slightly crooked, but the creature whisked it away before I could look a little closer.

"See how big your picture is in the brochure," he said next, handing me the programme. "You really look the part. Intelligent, spiritual, modest – humble and proud of it." He had slipped, and it gave me a jolt.

"How horrible," I said, aghast – humble and proud of it! Self-righteous people crucified Jesus! I took myself sternly in hand. What had I that I had not received? "And who gets prizes for gifts?" I asked myself sternly. I said I was sorry to Omnipotence and asked him to help me with the talk I was going to give.

"You don't need him to help you," remarked the snake in an offhand voice. "After all, you've given this talk so many times you could give it in your sleep! In fact, I could give it for you if you like."

"Go on then," I said, knowing he wouldn't. But his words troubled me. He was right. I had given this same message over and over again. But I was speaking to so many different groups by now it was hard to find the time to get other material ready. And so I gave the same message one more time. After the meeting, I felt quite good about it, until a lady walked up to me and said, "I've heard you speak twice before and each time you've said exactly the same things! Don't you have anything else to say?"

The snake choked. I went crimson with embarrassment and muttered defensively that maybe the Lord wanted to impress this message on her! Well, that did it. I felt absolutely miserable – and quite rightly so. "I told you you were famous," screamed the snake. "That's what you're famous for: your one talk." I spent a horrible evening and hardly felt as if I could go down to breakfast and face the woman the next morning.

"Well, Jill," Omnipotence said, "what about it? Do you have anything else to say?" I thought about it. To get a new series meant taking a risk. It also meant an additional investment of time, trouble, blood, sweat and tears. Other people used "one talk". Why couldn't I? I wondered.

"You can if you like," I seemed to hear Omnipotence saying, "but I would think you must be pretty bored with it by now." He was right and I knew it. What was more, I realised that if I was bored with the material, it wouldn't be long before I was boring everyone else to death with it, too. I needed to be teaching the same group of people on a regular basis. This way I would be forced to know, grow, and then I could go and sow! That made sense. I could take the best messages out of the different series I prepared and travel with them.

"My New Testament scribes take out of my treasure things that are familiar and things that are fresh," said Omnipotence. Well, I'd surely been flogging the familiar to death, I thought. It was high time I started work on the fresh! And so I made sure I was responsible and accountable to the same class of women every week. What a difference this made! The snake had certainly not intended his remarks to result in these sorts of decisions, so he tried again.

"You're famous," he said yet again, sliding up to me after a meeting in Grand Rapids. "See that man? That's Pat Zondervan of the Zondervan Corporation, and he wants to talk to you." Of course, he would never have pointed this out to me if he knew what was about to happen, but fortunately he isn't Omnipotence, so he doesn't know everything.

"Young lady, I would like that talk you just gave on my desk by September," Mr Zondervan said, smiling at me.

I gasped. "I can't write," I replied.

"She's right, she's right!" screeched the snake, writhing around in a terrible frenzy. "She's a ghastly speller. You'd have to pay your editors overtime, and her poor secretary would have to read her terrible scribble and ruin her eyesight. Why, she can't even type."

"Oh, shut up," I said. "I can't hear what Mr Zondervan is saying!"

"He really wants me to write," I told my husband when I got home.

"Then do it," Stuart said matter-of-factly.

"But I can't spell, and you know I can't even type." I caught myself in mid-sentence. I certainly didn't need to do the snake's work for him!

"Then do it longhand and use a dictionary," my husband was saying. "What does he want you to write about, anyway?" he asked.

"Well," I replied, "I think he just wants me to tell how I found out there was a snake in my garden."

Hell echoed with the shrieks of the demon chorus as the evil one thrashed about in fury. He had no idea the book was to be about him. He didn't care if I ignored him, and he didn't care if I got too interested in him. He did care if Omnipotence helped me get his number and told the world to watch out for him. "What are you going to call it?" Stuart was asking with interest.

"I've no idea," I said.

"Why not, *There's a Snake in My Garden*?" suggested my husband. And so the book was penned and arrived on Pat Zondervan's desk in September as he had asked.

The snake set about discouraging me as soon as the book came out. "No one will buy it, you know," he said. "For one thing, it's ridiculously overpriced. How can you let people pay all that money for your poverty-stricken little paperback when the starving millions are dying?"

Actually, the book did quite well. Mr Zondervan kindly asked me to write another one, then another, and another.

"You're famous," said a gushing lady to me a few years later. "Jill, how many books have you written?" I told her, ignoring the snake who was showing her the ones that had gone out of print that he had all lined up on his bookshelf! "Authors are so clever," the lady gushed on. "I wish I could get my book published. Would you possibly have time to read my manuscript?"

By now writing was a way of life for me. I wrote in the supermarket and I wrote on the plane. I wrote in the bedroom, living room, kitchen and conservatory, and even in the bathroom! I wrote at night and I wrote in the day. I wrote and wrote and wrote and the more I wrote, the more I was asked to write. *And I still couldn't type.*

"It's pathetic really," sniffed the snake. "You must be the only 'famous' Christian author I know who can't type. But then, everyone has to be famous for something." I giggled. I was glad I was a learner, a non-typing type of person who just tried her hardest to take the opportunity offered and do her best. I was glad I was famous for nothing very much, because that meant the good was left and the glory, if there was any, went to God.

God has his own ways of keeping my head regulation size, and it wasn't by fitting a halo around it either. "I love your book, *There's a Worm in My Soil*," a lady informed me enthusiastically.

"*There's a Snake in My Garden*," I corrected her gently.

"No, I haven't read that one," she replied briefly and moved on!

"I've really been greatly blessed by four of your books," another young woman confided.

"Really," I answered, "and where did you find them?" I expected her to answer "in a religious bookstore."

"In a garage sale," she replied without blinking an eyelid. Now that will keep anyone humble!

"Wonderful, really," the snake added, wickedly enjoying my reaction, "how people are 'led' to get rid of your books so others can be helped."

I tried to ignore him, but then I started to laugh again. "Dear Omnipotence," I prayed, "thank you, thank you, thank you for these wonderful ongoing reminders. I love it! Keep me famous for only one thing – my love for you and the ability never to take myself too seriously! And help me also to remember any skill I use for you is only borrowed for a time and is yours to give and yours to take away."

Omnipotence promised to make very, very sure that's exactly what would happen. "And now," he said, "let's write another book; go and sharpen your pencil."

"Writing gives me so many great opportunities," I told Stuart.

"Like what?" he asked me.

"Well," I said, "I was writing *Prime Rib and Apple* on a plane, and the man next to me said, 'You look as if you are writing a book.' 'I am,' I replied. 'So what's it about?' came the next question. 'Prime Rib and Apple,' I answered. 'Oh, a cookbook,' he said with interest. 'Hardly,' I was able to respond, 'although it's about mankind landing in a pretty pickle – or in the stew!'

"We had a great talk then," I said enthusiastically.

The snake was obviously getting fed up with both my books and the opportunities they were giving me to witness. He changed his tactics. If he couldn't stop my writing, he would try to distract me from the opportunities by the very activity itself – a favourite ploy.

My assignment was late. I had a chapter of a Bible study book to finish by the end of the week, and the end of the week had arrived. Fortunately, I had a plane flight that would afford me just about enough time to finish the job. Settling myself down in my seat, I began scribbling furiously, losing myself in the story of the Good Samaritan.

I pointed out how so many of us were like the priest and the Levite, riding along on our high horses above trouble, busy rushing to Bible studies at the temple. I noticed a young man watching me from across the aisle. He saw my notes and Bible, and I perceived his interest. I could tell even without looking up he wanted to engage me in conversation. "Don't stop," said the snake unexpectedly appearing from the seat pocket in front of me. "You know you have to get your assignments finished." I nodded and ignored the young man.

"Not only are we riding along on our evangelical donkeys," I wrote scathingly, "but there are men and women, boys and girls, lying in the ditch 'dying' for us to stop and attend to their wounds." The young man coughed and the snake hissed, "Go on, go on, write about getting down in the ditch; tell all those lazy, good-for-nothing Christians a thing or two they need to hear."

"What are you writing about?" the young man asked shyly. I looked up, not a little irritated at the interruption.

"Rude human," the snake sniffed, "deserves a rude answer. Don't you think?"

But Omnipotence had my eye. There was something about the young man's face. It was empty and sad. Sort of used up too young in life. "He's in the ditch, Jill," the Spirit of the Lord whispered in my ear. "Why don't you practise what you preach and get off *your* high horse?"

I shut my writing pad, turned toward the young man and realised with a shiver I had very nearly failed to complete my assignment of the day after all! It wasn't a chapter of a book at all; it was a chapter in the life of someone who would probably never read a Christian book, someone I was to discover needed a Good Samaritan to get down into his particular ditch and help him out.

"It's easy to become so absorbed by the 'work of the Lord' that you miss what the 'Lord of the work' is telling you to do," I told my husband that night. I certainly didn't want to be famous for that!

Writing books has certainly been a way of going where I could never go myself – multiplying the use for the material God has helped me to develop. And very importantly, writing has been a huge blessing to my own heart as well. Writing out my discoveries has forced me to inscribe the truth I am hoping to teach others deeply into my own mind and soul. I've also learned lots about myself. When I was asked to write *Wings*, a daily devotional, I discovered I was neither daily *nor* devotional, though I had fondly imagined I was. When I was invited to write an Easter and Christmas book for children, I was forced to break truth small enough for little minds to digest – very hard to do but exceedingly good for me. When I write about

Jesus, it is therapy, agony, ecstasy, and hopefully a literary experience that develops and shapes my soul into Christ's image. For this gift and opportunity I thank God!

25

The Big Five-O

It had come: my 50th birthday! I had done absolutely everything in my power to stop it arriving on the doorstep of my life, but it had ignored me. The snake was first to greet me with a huge birthday card with *50* written all over it in bright, clashing psychedelic colours. The *0* in the *50* was a picture of an old woman's wrinkled face with no teeth, little hair, and thick glasses. She was trying to smile; I wasn't even attempting to do the same.

Thirty had come and gone with little trauma – except a happy sort of expectation that I was now on the threshold of my most productive years. Forty had brought with it a little twinge of worry concerning the fleeting moments. "Where have all the years gone?" I wondered aloud to my husband. On my 50th, upon seeing my consternation as I opened all the cards (I was sure I had never received so many for my 20th, 30th or 40th; maybe my friends were worried they wouldn't get another chance), my husband said encouragingly (or so he thought), "Honey, what's the matter? Don't you believe you were born on the right day, that you've been moving at the right speed, and if you continue your innocuous progress, you'll be dead on time?" The snake appreciated the joke and was still laughing an hour later, while I didn't think it was funny at all. I thought about it, though.

Stuart was right, of course. And I did believe I had been born at the right time and would be "dead on time" as well, but believing it somehow brought little comfort. It wasn't even the 5–0 that worried me; it was what it represented. Thinking I would cheer myself up, I decided to go shopping. Walking through the door of the store, I tripped over a wheelchair just inside. I noticed the flick of a tail! Fancy his pushing it in my way. I apologised to the occupant.

"She looks very like you," the snake remarked pleasantly. "My, what beautiful silver hair!" I hurried by and bought myself a new blouse, ignoring the one offered to me by the reptile, beige and huge!

Was vanity my problem, I wondered? I'd always prided myself on not minding how "old" I looked. "Why start now?" I asked myself sternly. Feeling a little lift after purchasing my present to myself, I went into a café to get a good cup of tea. Still English at heart, I knew that tea was the panacea for all troubles. The snake had already taken the best seat and handed me a menu, pointing out a little box at the bottom of the card. I had not noticed it before, even though I frequented this particular café quite regularly. There was a caption at the top of the box that said, *senior citizens*. I snapped the menu shut, kicked the snake, and brooded into my cup of tea.

The aroma of the liquid in my cup caused me to dream about our life in England. I stopped abruptly when I realised that's what old folks do – dream about the past! I forced myself to think about the series of Bible studies I was preparing to teach. They were about Exodus and the three colourful figures of Moses, Aaron and Miriam.

"It's interesting, isn't it?" observed the snake, going along with my train of thought, "they were all over 80 years of age." Funnily enough, that started my mind going in a direction the snake had absolutely not intended.

"It's true," I replied. "In fact, God didn't even call Moses to his life's work until he was 80 years of age. And then there were Anna and Simeon in the New Testament. They saw Jesus with their own eyes at the *end* of their lives, not the beginning!" Come to think of it, age really seemed to be irrelevant to God. After all, he is the Ancient of Days and has counted out our moments for us, keeping the best to come for another day in another place. What's more, he intends to be as present and faithful to us in any one day as much as another.

Then I began to get a handle on my problem. It wasn't so much a panic that I was into the last one-third of my life, as a realisation that reality must be faced. I had caught myself thinking, "When I grow up, I want to be…" And my birthday brought home the fact that I *had* grown up and I would never *be* some of those things I had dreamt about.

Like a Bible school student, for example. Never having had the chance to go full-time to a seminary or Bible school, I realised that now I never would. "Face it, Jill," I lectured myself. I had always wanted to travel to disaster areas, to refugee camps, and work giving out food and life-saving drugs. I would never be able to do that now either. My ailing back wouldn't let me. I would never translate the Bible into an unknown language either, or write the series of books I'd always believed I'd one day have time to write. I was mourning the things I would never do for Jesus. "You've missed it, haven't you?" intoned the snake, appearing suddenly at my side. "Pity!"

Omnipotence reminded me kindly that I could still study at any level I wanted to with the wonderful layman's tools available to me, and I was privileged to be on the board of World Relief, one of the most effective relief agencies in the world. That position gave me a chance to give strategic input into refugee and hunger problems all over the globe. What's more, he reminded me, Stuart and I were going to speak to Wycliffe translator's missionary conference that summer where *all* the missionaries from that field would be gathered together. I suddenly saw that I wouldn't have had any of these wonderful opportunities *unless* I was 50!

"Some privileges wait for us to grow up, don't they?" I said aloud in the direction of the snake who jumped off the seat next to me and disappeared. I returned home to be met by my "younger than ever"-looking husband (he's five years older than me) who greeted me with a kiss that made me feel anything but 50! Over a candlelight dinner he encouraged me with phrases like "accumulated wisdom" and "hard-earned experience" and urged me to use the milestone to plan my time and energy a little more strategically. He pointed out that the worldwide opportunities we were being graciously given were there for the choosing and taking. We just needed to stay in touch with him who said, "I have placed before you an open door that no one can shut" (Revelation 3:8). It was a wonderful evening.

The next day a man arrived to sell some carpeting for a room we were renovating. He showed me the samples. "This will last 40 years," he said, showing me the most expensive sample.

"Take the one that will only last fifteen," advised the snake, sniggering. "Why waste your money or leave it for your children?"

I managed to ignore him and chose the one that would last 30! If I were still here to enjoy it at the age of 80, I mused, that would be ten more years than I had been promised anyway. Didn't the Bible say, "The length of our days is 70 years – or 80, if we have the strength" (Psalm 90:10).

It hadn't done me any harm at all to have a birthday – even such a strategic one. In fact, having it gave me a strategic look at that very strategic word, *strategic*. It was time to put all I was doing under scrutiny and ask the Lord to help me decide what part of all the "all" I was doing needed to be relegated to the "some" of the all I did!

"How can I maximise my time and energy?" I mused.

"Retire and pray?" suggested the snake, hopefully. He meant *retire*; he had no intention of letting me pray, but it sounded pious. "You've done your part in the church," he advised, trying to sound wise. "Let the 'younger' ones take over now. You can potter round your garden, visit retirement centres to encourage the dying, and..." He watched me bending down to tie my shoelace. "Can you think of anything else you could do while you're down there?" he ended wickedly!

I straightened up with difficulty and made note of the fact that my body certainly was shouting for a change of pace, but as usual the snake had overstepped (or rather, over-slithered) himself. He had actually focused my attention on the *urgency* and preciousness of time and therefore the necessity for being corrective, selective, and effective! I mean if I was indeed in the last third of my life – and who knew just how far *into* the last third I was – then I'd better make better choices between options where my service for the Lord was concerned.

I promised the Lord I would give it all I'd got in the time I had left and set to planning my 50s as thoroughly as he had helped me plan the 20s and 30s. "Make me a force to be reckoned with for you in the coming decade, Jesus," I prayed. "May 50 be the start of the most spiritually productive years of my life." Funny, when I put my birthday cards on the mantelpiece that evening, the one with the ugly psychedelic colours that didn't match and the old woman's face was gone!

26

A GRANDmother

couldn't believe it. The snake was curled up, biting his lip (very dangerous for a snake), and trying to be creative. Now he's always wanted to be like God, so this was really no surprise. "I'm writing you a poem," he said smugly.

Despite myself I was interested. "What's it about?" I asked hesitantly.

"It's about your becoming a GRANDmother," he said with a huge emphasis on the GRAND. I knew I shouldn't even look at his nasty little poem, but I was nosey and wanted to know what he'd written. He handed me the paper and I read:

A GRANDmother, not her, how wild
when yesterday she was but child
My connotations of the name
are "dehydrated, yellowed, lame."

A GRANDMOTHER, not her, not she
when grew she up past 33?
I can't recall they asked permission
to put her in this strange position.

A GRANDPARENT, whatever gender
sounds like a car with bended fender!

It even rhymed, and I couldn't help feeling it *did* reflect a few of my thoughts and feelings. After all, how *could* someone as young as I was be old enough to be a "grandMOTHER"?

"I think 'GRANDmother' sounds better," the snake insisted. "Such a *suitable* name." He handed me my glasses. "By the way," he added casually, "I see they're coming out with those Bibles with *huge* print!"

I thought about my children and the excited transatlantic phone call that had thrilled us to bits. "Dad, Mum, you're going to be grandparents!"

"That's what I mean in my poem," the snake confided earnestly. "Why, one day you were a perfectly normal mother, and the next day, with not so much as a 'by your leave' they make you a 'GRANDone'."

I'd had enough of the slimy thing. Snatching the pencil out of his hand, I finished his poem for him.

Bent out of shape by this grand title,
I'd like to kick against life's cycle!
Unless I see beyond the name
the miracle of One who came
to light my life and give me reason
to welcome this grandmothering season!

A piece of broad eternity
Just for my sweet grandchild and me.
I'll tell him all about my Lord
About his shoulders bent and broad.
Yet large enough to bear the weight
of all our sin and all our hate.
I'll tell him all about his hands
so torn with briars of death's demands,
And what it cost to "follow me"
to such extreme calamity.
I'll tell him Jesus will him keep
till he grows up to be a sheep!

The snake choked with rage and slithered away – for a season. As I talked to the Lord about this new incredible thing that was about to happen not only to our beautiful children but to us, it was Jesus who helped me adjust and who reminded me that the 20s were not necessarily for running, the 30s for walking, the 40s for sitting, and the 50s for rocking!

The Lord helped me to see: *A piece of broad eternity. Just for my sweet grandchild and me.* Suddenly I was filled with a huge sense of privilege and excitement as God let me peep around the corner of tomorrow. "What a blessing to be alive to 'peep' in the first place," I thought. My own experience had been that three of my four grandparents had died before I was born. I did get to know the one living grandpa, and what a joy that short encounter proved to be for both of us. Stuart's father had in fact died just four weeks before Dave, our first child, arrived, and my own father a few years before that, so they both missed the privilege.

Then I thought about the opportunity I would have to tell our grandchildren about Christ. One of my fondest memories of my earliest days is story time on my grandfather's knees. Not only could I start collecting some excellent Christian books I knew were available, I could even write some!

The snake appeared immediately. He hates children. "You couldn't write a children's book if you tried for a whole year," he jeered derisively. He was probably right, I reflected, but I went ahead and tried anyway, and enjoyed it so much I kept right on going.

So this grand-sheep (I like that title a lot better than grandmother) set about happily getting to know this incredible little person who threw me for a loop by appearing on the scene – my scene. He helped me adjust just in time to welcome number two in a veteran manner – *Hallelujah!* Anyone want to see my pictures?

"I don't," said the snake, appearing out of nowhere again. Of course I didn't expect the snake to be interested in my adorable photos, but everyone else would surely want to see them. And why not? I thought smugly. Weren't they the most gorgeous GRANDchildren ever?

I found myself adding one more *very* strategic event to my busier-than-ever calendar: time with Danny and Michael. If I were going to bond with these precious little boys, and all the other little ones yet unborn, I knew it would take quality time spent together. Not easy when they lived a state away. But it could be *made* to happen, I decided.

"Interfering thing," the snake sniffed. "Why do you think those children of yours want you hanging around all the time? They want to bring their family up *their* way not *yours*. Not that they're right, of course," he added hastily, seeing an obvious opportunity to sow some seeds of tension between the generations. "Why don't you tell them to get the little beggars on a tighter schedule like you had them on when they were young? I mean, last time you were there I remember you went to bed *very* late, and Danny and Michael said good night to you and tucked you into bed!" He was twisting the truth as usual, but these young people of ours certainly had a different way of doing things, I mused.

I learned to invite myself at *helpful* times and always to try to give the young parents some relief time together. "Why don't you take your wife out for a meal *without* the tribe," I'd suggest. And when Judy and Greg's first child appeared on the scene in the same 48 hours as Dave and Deb's twins, I took a baby sabbatical and divided my attention between them. What joy!

I found a whole new world had opened up to me. How was it I had never noticed how many GRANDchildren there were in the world before? They were all over the place. Now I smiled indulgently on the plane when one sat next to me, giving me a chance to talk to the young mother and help her with the mountain of paraphernalia, seemingly essential for the task when you travel with a baby.

What fun it was to stand in the church lobby and greet the little ones with their mothers, instead of the mothers with their little ones! And what fun to be blissfully "detached" when one or another of our near-perfect little ones acted up in a public place. After all, these were my children's children, not mine, which seemed a good enough reason for me to ignore their tantrums, smile indulgently, and watch my frustrated children try to cope. "Badly behaved little horrors," commented the snake. "You can see they're headed for a life of crime!"

I laughed. They certainly underlined my belief in original sin. After all, I knew no one had taught them how to do all those naughty little things they seemed perfectly adept at doing. Somehow they knew how to do all the wrong things perfectly naturally, all by themselves. But I reminded the snake, "Jesus loves them, this I know" and hummed the little tune knowing he couldn't abide it. It would only be a matter of time before this second generation grasped the incredible thing that Jesus had done for them and responded.

I sighed. "It's hard," I said to Omnipotence, "knowing there will be a snake in their gardens, too." There seemed to be so many more horrible dangers in their world than there had been when our children were growing up. I thought back to our garden in England and how we always left our babies outside in their prams all by themselves – sometimes for hours.

"You can't do that here," Debbie said to me wistfully. "Child snatchers are a horrible nightmarish reality. Even in a store you have to watch them like a hawk."

I remembered how the street children we had worked with handled our children and how they made great big brothers and sisters for them. Then I listened to some of our friends in youth work who had terrible dilemmas worrying about the children they were trying to help and about their own children and how safe they all were in neighbourhoods that might have a strong gang presence.

I thought about my son's statement that eight out of nine babies born in the hospital the same night as his twins were born to single mothers, and I realised if the predictions were correct, that our grandchildren stood a good chance of marrying girls and boys who would bring lots of damage from their pasts along with them into their marriages. Yes, it was a different world. It would also cost thousands of pounds more to educate them. However would our pastor sons manage?

The snake played unrelentingly with these thoughts, supplying me with mind movie after mind movie – most X-rated and featuring our little ones as the victims.

"Think about the opportunities though," suggested Stuart when I voiced some of my fears. "Yes, it's a terrible world, but what a start these children have. Temptation isn't only a chance to do wrong but a chance to do right! They have wonderful Christian parents and a loving church environment. They have GRANDparents that love, pray and intend to influence them as thoroughly as they influenced their own, and a God who fully promises and intends to lend us all the expertise we need to get this parenting job done. Imagine the challenge of the 21st century," he continued, warming to his theme. "There have never been such resources and global opportunities to take the whole gospel to the whole world as in this coming generation."

"There have never been so many martyrs up to now either," hissed the snake.

I was able to look up, turn my eyes upon Jesus, and see him smiling down at me. This was his world, he reminded me. He was perfectly capable of caring for his own. I could leave all my loved ones in his hands! He wouldn't drop them. "No man could pluck them out of the Father's hands."

I knew it. What a GRAND promise for GRANDparents for their GRANDchildren, from a GRAND GOD who is as great and as grand as his Word.

27

God is Good,
All the Time

"Oh, I never expected this!" my friend said, tears streaming down her face. I talked long and earnestly with her, assuring her that God was indeed good all the time. Even when things were bad.

"Life goes on. Yes, it does," I said earnestly. "Like the tide, life comes in and life goes out inexorably day by daily day. There are bad tides and good tides. Rip tides and gentle tides. High tides and low tides. But the shore stays the same. We can't stop life breaking over us like the tide, but we can bank on God being the same."

My friend gave me a strange look. I felt bad immediately, realising that her daughter's three-year marriage had just been dissolved. There had been a divorce. How could I have been so thoughtless?

At once, the snake was in evidence to rub it in. "Your

words sounded smug and sanctimonious," he accused me. "What do you know about it?" I was lost for anything to say. He was right. The devil is often right – but only when it suits him, of course. Being the Father of lies, he constantly twists the truth; but occasionally – very occasionally – he uses truth to meet his own ends. Perhaps he knew that soon the shoe would be on the other foot.

"Is God good all the time, Jill?" my friend asked again.

"Yes," I replied stubbornly, "even when things are bad." I shivered. Somewhere I could hear sardonic laughter.

She left then, and I sat thinking about the conversation we had had. I felt that chill wind blowing, somewhere deep down in my soul. Near at hand – too near at hand – I heard the hiss of a snake.

I was sad about my friend's pain. We had children that had grown up at the church together. They were good friends. They had sung in the youth choir and gone on short-term missions. It was not a good match when her daughter fell in love and married a boy she met at the university. All of us, except her daughter, seemed to know it. Now, three short years later, the boy was gone, shacking up with one of the daughter's friends on the other side of the city. There was one small, bewildered two-year-old girl left in the mess. For some reason that she couldn't understand, Daddy had disappeared.

I thought about our own children, all happily married and in Christian ministry. Suddenly I was grateful for this amazing blessing. I realised, with some apprehension, that I had taken it far too much for granted, though it was quite unthinkable to me that any disaster such as had visited my friend would ever visit our tent. Divorce was horrible, but it belonged to other people's stories, not ours. It certainly was happening to many people, including a growing number in our own church family. Our fellowship was growing in leaps and bounds, but as it grew, the biggest headache emerging was the divorce situations that began to abound.

Subconsciously, I realise now, I believed this happened to other people's children, not to ours; ours were surely safe. After all, they loved Jesus and were all in ministry. Again, somewhere far too near for comfort, the hiss was unmistakable. The temperature unexplainably cooled. I shivered and went home.

It must haven been a short few months after this conversation that I received a phone call from our daughter. The hissing was back. I stood transfixed, with that horrible hissing noise drowning out the impossible-to-believe words from a daughter in floods of tears. The words were stark. Her brother, and our beloved first-born, a young pastor in his first church, had just watched his wife of over fourteen years walk out of the parsonage door, taking our four beautiful grandchildren with her.

Shaking, I put the phone down and got on my knees. He was there in a flash. I saw him in a new light. Triumphant and cruel, he stared at me malevolently. He hated us all. He hated Stuart and he hated me. He hated our children, each and every one of them. And he loathed our little ones. He would never change his mind about us. He couldn't change his mind. The devil is fixed evil. He is real – as real as you and I – and he means business. Bad business. He was on a serious, diabolical, search and destroy mission, and had managed to win a round with his arch-Enemy, hands down.

"You're right to be angry," he said indignantly, trying to get me to accuse the Lord of neglect. "Just where was 'you know who' (he could never bear to say that hated name out loud) when your poor little boy needed him? I bet you never expected this sort of treatment! Haven't you served him faithfully all these years? This is a nice way to say thank you!"

But I knew I must stop letting him talk to me. I had to stop listening. I needed to tell him in Jesus' name to go away! I asked the Lord to deal with him and tell him where to go, and reached for my Bible.

For a long time I hung my heart over the Word of God, on that dark and terrible day. I was weeping and gasping in emotional pain the like of which I had never in my life experienced. I was simply saying over and over: "Jesus, help us; Jesus, tell me this is a nightmare and I'll wake up and find this could not possibly be happening to us. Jesus, Saviour, help us – save us." Then, as I let the soothing balm of God's dynamic word flow over me, calmness came. I realised I was in for some learning; some soul exercises I had never before experienced.

The snake can no more abide the presence of someone calling desperately on God's wonderful holy name than fly to the moon. He also can't abide staying around when you read the Bible, though he sometimes tries to misquote what you are reading. This time he left me alone for a while.

I eventually got off my knees, where I had been reading God's word, wiped the tears away and went to sit before the Lord. How long I was there I don't know, but suddenly the words I had given so glibly to my friend months ago flooded back to my mind. "God is good – *all* the time." And then her words – *"Oh, I never expected this!"* – came rushing unbidden back to me. I decided to take my own advice.

I repeated out loud: "God is good, all the time – all the time – *all the time* – ALL THE TIME." I knew, with a sudden inner certainty, that I must not get God and life mixed up. "Life is bad – *but* God is good." I repeated it all day, till my husband came home that night. Whenever I heard that infernal hissing, I would start to use the name of Jesus and ask him to deal with him, and I found the "noise" died away. After that I left my Bible open on the kitchen table, and as I went about my duties in the house I would read a verse or two in passing and comfort my raw spirit with its soothing words.

That first most incredible night, when my husband and I just sat and looked at each other, trying to process the news, my man simply said to me, "This must not drive a wedge between us, Jill. Let's tell the Lord and promise each other this will only serve to drive us together and not break us apart!"

The snake had sneaked back. "What a strange thing to say to you," he whispered. Never had he looked so frightening to me. Never had he sounded so menacing. He noticed my new respect for him with evil delight. Gone were the "angel of light" phenomena he so often used with me, to draw away my suspicions and lull me into a false sense of security. I was frightened of him in a way I had never been frightened of him before. Had I allowed myself to grow complacent where Satan and all his demons were concerned? I think so. Had I somehow been proud enough to imagine I had him tagged? That I could handle any of his horrible little schemes? Had I underestimated his considerable power and ability to sow unfaithfulness, betrayal and horrible pain, death and corruption all over the world and, more precisely, *my* world? I found myself exclaiming, "Lord, I never expected this!"

"Why not?" the snake asked me craftily. "Why should you, Jill Briscoe, be exempt? Why should your children be little goodie two shoes and always do what's right? Who do you think you are; who do you think they are?"

Then I thought again about Stuart's words: "We won't let this drive us apart." What did he mean?

The snake said in a trice, "He means you aren't going to agree on how to handle this. This will probably destroy *your* marriage too. Don't you remember the family whose little boy developed leukaemia? They got a divorce. They couldn't agree on the treatment."

When I questioned Stuart on what he had meant, he answered: "The couple with the little boy with leukaemia didn't use their pain to drive them to God or into each other's arms. They allowed it to divide them. We will stand together on this."

"Two are better than one, it says in Ecclesiastes," I replied resolutely. "That's what it will be like with us."

"No – no – no," I heard far away. But I left God to deal with him and turned my mind to my part in the situation we found ourselves in. "Oh, I never expected this," I distinctly heard the snake hiss! He had expected us to collapse under the blow.

The nightmare continued, and despite prayer and perseverance, our story ended in a heart-breaking divorce. Four little children, frightened and helpless, were divided up by a stranger in a sterile courtroom, our former daughter-in-law being given custody.

"What justice!" screamed the snake, delighted with the outcome. "That's the court system for you. You'll never see your grandchildren now! Of course," he added subtly, "you could try going to the supermarket in the hope she's shopping and has taken the children along!"

The weary years passed. God was good *all the time*. Life stank, but God was good! I repeated it to myself, day by day by day by day! So did our son. His deep bedrock faith in his God, the Rock of his salvation, never wavered, though his faith in people took a massive hit. But he refused to get God and life mixed up.

This was not what the snake was hoping for. He had tried his best to get us all mad at God. Disappointed with him. And, of course, he wanted to make us angry at each other too. He wanted us mad at everyone in sight. With me, he worked on fanning the flames of anger at my former daughter-in-law. Anger at the man who had enticed my daughter-in-law into sin. He continued to try to divide my husband and me. But God helped us to hate what people were doing, but to recognise that they weren't the enemy – the snake was!

He tried another tack. He never gives up, you know. "Now, next," he said, "let's see how you handle this in front of your congregation. They are expecting you to smile and lie about it all – telling everyone 'God is good, all the time' – when you're really as mad as anything at him and his neglect in not keeping your precious children wrapped in cotton wool."

"God is good, all the time," I whispered stubbornly. I added, "Jesus, please deal with the snake for us." At the mention of his dear name, the snake was gone. He cannot abide the slightest mention of any one of his names. Especially the "Jesus – Saviour" one!

I was learning that my helplessness could be my greatest asset: my weapon of warfare against despair and hopelessness; against fading faith. Helplessness is, after all, the basis of all prayer. As we cast ourselves on God, he lifts our head and gives us faith to go on going on.

I was learning that Jesus didn't only die for what we have done – and we are all sinners: "there is none righteous, no not one" – but he died for all we have not done, too! There are sins of commission, and sins of omission.

It didn't take long before the snake, waiting till my guard was down, crawled back into my mind to tell me that if I'd been a better mother and taught my boy to be a better husband ("He must have done something wrong; it takes two, you know"), then this wouldn't have happened. A heavy blanket of mother-guilt lay over my life that day.

I hadn't been a perfect mum, and I knew it. "If only..." I began to think. The snake loves "If only" words. He swishes his tail in delight and screeches, "More! More!"

Don't let him encourage you to play his game. "If only" helps no one. Put your guilt-generated "if onlys" at the foot of the cross, where they belong, and get on with being the person you need to be right now! Fight him on all fronts and ask God how and where you can work towards damage control!

None of us have been the parent we should have been. But we should not let that stop us being the parent we need to be. "You didn't do it all right, Jill, true," the Lord said to me on that guilt-ridden day. "But you didn't do it all wrong, either."

The snake had disappeared. The Lord's word always has that effect on him. "Why don't we read it aloud to the snake more?" I wondered, watching his hasty disappearing act. I was free, once he had gone, to talk to the Lord about my regrets. He reminded me that I was a fallen mother, with fallen children who married other fallen children, and we all lived in a fallen world, in a fallen culture, with hosts of fallen angels helping us all to fall on and on and on, so what did I expect?

I wondered how I could have said, as my friend had said in her dark day, "Oh, I never expected this!" Hadn't Jesus himself told his disciples: "In the world you *will* have tribulation; *but* be of good cheer, I have overcome the world" (John 16:33, NKJV)? But Jesus had also prayed that day to his heavenly Father: "I do not pray that you should take them out of the world, but that you should keep them from the evil one" (John 17:15, NKJV).

Yes, I thought, "Greater is he that is in us than he that is in the world." So I said, very loudly, so he could hear me: "Even though none of us does it all right (mothering, or anything else), none of us does it all wrong, either!"

Now, years later, this terrible thing that happened to our family is no less a terrible thing, but God has been able to redeem some of the mess. Not all of the mess, but some of it. He is a God of Grace. All Grace. And he is good *all the time*!

He has "restored many of the years the locusts have eaten". Not all of the years, but many of the years. He has made us all better ministers of the gospel of grace because of it. Our firstborn married again – a lovely servant of the Lord who had herself suffered a divorce – and they both began to rebuild their lives and their family. They began to have a ministry to blended families and, with time, with their children restored, set about parenting with a heart. The children responded.

Our congregation looked at us differently from that day on. We realised we now understood much of the heart-pain of too many of our own people. "Now you understand," their kind eyes said. "Help us," they asked. "Comfort us with the same comfort God is giving you."

Reading the story of Joseph and his brothers not long ago, I came across the wonderful words of this man so dreadfully treated by his family. As he forgave his brothers for selling him into slavery, he said: "You meant it for evil, but God meant it for good."

Those words reverberated round hell that day, even as words of faith do today when we can refuse to charge God with wrongdoing, realise who our enemy is and get on with life. Our great enemy is the snake, not people. I also understand a little better that the snake, whatever disguise he adopts, is hellish and fiendish, and we in our own strength are no match for him. Only by hiding in the names of Jesus – claiming his blood as a covering, and in dependence and faith using his word to thoroughly defeat the enemy – can we triumph over all his evil schemes and turn tragedy into the triumph of the cross. God is good, *all the time*! Life isn't always good, but God always is. Bank on it!

28

Stepping Out

"How can someone as young as me be as old as this?" my bewildered husband asked me. It was his 70th birthday. The snake inserted his unasked-for opinion into the wondering silence. He had brought along an AARP (American Association of Retired Persons) catalogue and was showing us the pages of retirement homes in Florida.

"It's high time you were wrapping up this church thing," he said, trying to sound sincerely concerned for us. "You've done a wonderful job, but my word, you're *70* years of age! God isn't a taskmaster, you know. He wants to reward you with a nice rest now. Like a 'total' rest – like a rest from all the hectic spiritual stuff you've been overloading yourself with these last few years. Maybe you should step *out*…" (What he wanted to say was, "Maybe you should step *over* – over a cliff or some such precipice, and put your poor congregation out of their misery!") But Stuart interrupted him. I don't know if he even heard him.

"Maybe it's time for a younger man to take over – I'm concerned about staying too long."

The snake was ecstatic. "Bad thing, that," he agreed vehemently. "It could be you've stayed too long already. I heard some of your so-called 'loyal' parishioners talking in the parking lot and distinctly heard words like 'old man, decrepit, fading, losing it'. Why don't you sell up, get out of ministry and just play golf?"

"I can't imagine just playing golf," Stuart said gloomily, as if he had heard the wretched thing. The snake hurriedly corrected himself.

"Oops! I didn't mean golf; what about watching football all day, then?" Seeing a light coming into my football-loving husband's eyes, he continued: "Imagine watching all the football you want to – all day, every day – doing nothing else from morning till night. So much football you wouldn't have time to do the old stuff; things like studying that old Bible of yours, or filling in in the pulpit when the next reverend has taken over – you need to stop being obsessed with ministry, you know; being carried away with the idea that the church can't do without you."

"I don't think you're fading at all!" I said loudly. "Your preaching is better than I've ever heard you. People are coming to Christ, believers are being strengthened, and students are hearing God's call through you. You are like a 60-year-old, not a 70-year-old! Perhaps you should consider stepping out – to take on a special project or something – but not stepping down from ministry. Maybe we should ask the Lord how we can best use our last years together, strategically, to make the devil sorry he started the whole mess in the first place!" The snake hissed, and we got excited!

"Maybe we should pray about it," my husband answered. That was it! The snake threw an absolute conniption. Of course, I knew why. As the little couplet says:

The devil trembles when he sees
The weakest saint upon his knees.

That's because he knows where the power is, of course. Power comes in faithful spiritual warfare with the enemy of our souls. Whatever else happens, he has to stop us praying. Stop us shaping our worries into prayers. Stop us turning our dilemmas into questions for God, or anything else that comes near any sort of spiritual warfare at all. It sends him right over the edge.

"Just use your common sense," the snake resumed, returning to the subject in hand. "You're past it; admit it. Fading – yes – definitely fading. I mean, you're an old traditionalist. Really old-fashioned. Out of touch – and who can blame you at your age? No one under 50 is going to give you the time of day any more. You're 70 years old – and you've done a fine job for your master" (he always said the word "master" through clenched teeth). "Now it's time to step out," he almost shouted. "Out of ministry – out of preaching – out of evange-lism." He could hardly get the hated words out of his horrid little snake mouth; but he managed it. There was too much at stake not to fling in every argument; to put us off what was beginning to be clear. There was something else God had for us to do in ministry. We were not finished yet.

As the days went on, we became aware somehow, deep down in our souls, that something big was looming ahead. Gifts didn't age and hearts didn't age, and we were ready for whatever was coming down the highway.

"Well," said my husband, apparently ignoring the snake's distractions, "I'm going to speak at this conference in the Philippines next week. It's on the growth of the church in the developing world" (where, I knew, the church is growing exponentially, but there are not enough hands to the pump). "Maybe I'll learn something that will help us to make a decision about what the Lord wants for the rest of our lives."

The snake hurriedly packed his horrid little bag of tricks – a terrorist bomb and mask – an AK47 and a bottle of spiritual lethargy – and booked a flight to the Philippines.

Once safely there (the snake's bag of tricks was useless, as the Master wanted the plane full of pastors to attend the conference, and had his guardian angels all around the plane as it flew through the devil's territory), Stuart settled in to learn what God was doing around the world. Meanwhile, I reflected how we are really safe down here on earth only when we are in the centre of God's will, and he who counts out our days is the Lord, not the snake. We don't go to heaven one minute before we are meant to. See Psalm 139:16!

My husband got busy teaching the Bible readings in the morning and settled in to learn all he could about the urgent needs of the church in the developing world. There are so many pastors out there with no biblical training at all. Many cannot even read or write. What is more, they never would have any training or education, because it wasn't available to them, and if it had been available they couldn't afford it. Even if they could have afforded it, they could never get away from their work long enough to do it.

The speaker challenged the people at the convention. "What we need are people who will devote themselves to bringing informal Bible training to this world, where they are crying out like the man of Macedonia: come over and help us!"

Sitting in the rows among the leaders who had come from all over the world for this event, the snake and his cohorts watched in dismay as many contributed their wisdom, experience and ideas to try to solve the problem. How could the world church combine resources and finish the job, begun over 2,000 years ago, of bringing in the Kingdom?

The snake was slowly being driven crazy watching it all happen. "Look at that," he hissed to his cohorts, watching my 70-year-old husband carefully. "His heart is strangely warmed! It's a call on his life; *a call on his life*;" (his voice rising to a shriek) "A CALL ON HIS LIFE! How can the Enemy do that to him at his age? And how can his wretched servant obey him – just like that?" But he had lost the battle, and he knew it.

Joining me in South Africa shortly after this, Stuart told me what had happened to him at the conference. "Jill, I think I've had another call. There is another task waiting. Another mountain to climb. We can help. We can do this. You and I are informally biblically trained. We understand these emerging leaders. We have learned by 'doing'. We learned how to learn and go on learning and never stop. We can help these men and women to do the same."

Back in Wisconsin, Stuart announced that after 30 years as their Senior Pastor he was stepping down – not out of ministry – but from being Senior Pastor. Stepping out into the biggest challenge of our lives. Not stepping down; stepping up. Higher and higher, "making full proof of our ministry". A worldwide challenge and calling lay ahead of us. We would simply make ourselves available to answer invitations of anyone who needed us to help. If we were free, we would go – anywhere, anytime – to encourage and strengthen the arm of a new and exciting emerging church in the developing world.

Our friends who loved us were concerned. Our children were apprehensive. Our enemies attributed motives to us that were not particularly flattering! But the call was insistent and very real, and on both of us. What a thrill to believe that this last lap of the good race would be run together! The Christian never retires from ministry. Maybe from employment. Maybe from a paid position on a church or mission staff. But never from being a disciple of Jesus Christ, a disciple who has promised to follow him to the end – whenever the end will be.

It has been a wild ride. Eight years of world-wide travel. Seven years of finding ourselves in difficult places with difficult cultures, and often among difficult people! Seven years of meeting God's best servants, often living in impossible situations yet refusing to do anything but tell the gospel and love the Lord Jesus, whatever happens to them and whatever happens to their children as a result. We have seen churches planted where there were no churches; converts made who have been the first in a whole country to hear about Jesus and his love. We have found ourselves in the right place at the right time to counsel and build up battered servants of God. We have preached to thousands – or to two or three persecuted believers. We have watched our books being translated into the languages of the communist countries by the communists themselves! Books like Stuart's *The Ten Commandments: The Liberating Rules of God*, in Beijing, China; or others in African, South American or Eastern European tongues. I have had the privilege of editing a magazine for women in leadership and ministry wives that has spread to over 70 countries.

We have been frightened and we have been weary. We have been accepted and loved and appreciated, as well as being greeted with suspicion and hostility. We have been on all seven continents and flown millions of miles. We have longed for our children and our childrens' children, and have been so grateful for the brief times allowed to touch and hug, listen, love, cry and support one another.

The snake has been along for the ride, of course. We are never finished with him down here. He will be with us till we see Jesus face to face. But we, in our old age, have grown a little more adept at recognising his voice and letting the Master answer his insidious questions and help us to overcome his temptations. We have learned that temptation is not only a chance to go wrong but an opportunity to go right. To be strengthened in our faith. To grow goodness in our lives.

And we have watched new converts overcome him in the name of Jesus and in the power of their God. We have also seen the devastation he has wrought in God's good earth, as he knows his time is short and is making the best of it (or rather the worst of it), and we have come to understand his terrible determination to kill anything in his path he can kill. He is out to destroy people's hopes, dreams, faith, family relationships and marriages. He is in deadly earnest, and we trivialise him at our peril. But we have also learned that the victory is ours in Jesus, and we need not be alarmed or dismayed. In the words of Martin Luther:

And though this world, with devils filled,
Should threaten to undo us;
We will not fear, for God hath willed
His truth to triumph through us.

Surely, as Luther promises us, "One little word shall fell him." And what is that little word? It is no "little" word at all. It is Jesus, Jesus, Jesus. *That* is the word that strikes terror into the devil's heart. Of course, he has no "heart" – just a mind, twisted, terrible and intent on destroying all his Enemy holds dearest. You and me. Jesus-lovers and glory-givers all. Lovers of righteousness and soldiers of the cross. Servants of him who is supreme.

Yes, the snake may be the prince of the power of the air. But Jesus is the *King*! Hallelujah!

29

Perspective

"Let's get ourselves into perspective, shall we?" said my Lord. "Never forget – you're nothing more than a little dust, Lady. Do you know that? 'Dust thou art, and to dust shalt thou return.'"

I thought about that and wrote the following:

Dust cannot be **independent**. *Dust is* **dependent** *on a supernatural force to keep it sticking together, and we are told who that force is. The Bible says by him all things consist. God laughs as he listens to dust talk.*

Talk that says:
I don't need *God.*
My own self-sufficiency will keep
me from falling apart
my own **dust mind,**
Dust abilities.
In the words of a well-known song: **I'm strong,**

I'm invincible, I'm woman!
And God says: **Puff!**
And dust flies away!

A little dust person is dependent on climate, on dust food and shelter, and on dust health.

Germs love dust. It's a lifelong battle to keep them at bay.

God is perfect health. He has never been sick in one moment of eternity.

But little dust people prefer to rely on bottles of dust pills advertised on dust television. They seldom ask the *source of health* to shine *his* rays into their dust bodies and, if it be his will, heal their diseases.

Dust thinks it can figure out the universe, understand all mysteries, solve all riddles, and ingeniously has learned to manipulate atoms so it can blow up all the other little dust people in the world.

But God loves his little dust people. They are his idea. He wants to reconcile them to himself so they can discover his best. Held together by his power – secure in his keeping – he longs to bless them so much that he placed an ever-living spirit within them and planned a resurrection body that would never disintegrate. It would even have the ability to live God's sort of life with him.

God wanted to be sure the dust people understood the plan of salvation, so he came himself and lived in a dust body for a time so he could tell them about his wonderful plan *personally*.

Some dust got very angry and tried to blow him apart, but other little men, women and children who knew they were but dust clung to him and acknowledged freely their absolute dependence on

The source of their being,
Creator and sustainer of their life,
Saviour of their souls.

When the dust bodies were laid in dust boxes, their spirits went at once to be with him in heaven's home.

Proud dust, watch out!
Dust thou art, and unto dust shalt thou return.
Humble dust, blessed art thou.
Dependent dust, he will not disappoint you.
One day, glorified dust you will be!

This little piece of dependent dust thought about that last line, "Glorified dust you will be!" And suddenly I thought of something else. On that glorious day, *there won't be a snake in my garden!*

Alleluia!

Made in the USA
Middletown, DE
31 May 2018